Chess Endgame
Workbook for Kids

John Nunn

THE LONE
KING

GAMBIT

First published in the UK by Gambit Publications Ltd 2020

ISBN-13: 978-1-911465-38-6
ISBN-10: 1-911465-38-4

DISTRIBUTION:
Worldwide (except USA): Central Books Ltd, 50 Freshwater Road, Chadwell Heath, London RM8 1RX, England. Tel +44 (0)20 8986 4854 Fax +44 (0)20 8533 5821.
E-mail: orders@Centralbooks.com

Gambit Publications Ltd, 50 Freshwater Road, Chadwell Heath, London RM8 1RX, England.
E-mail: info@gambitbooks.com
Website (regularly updated): www.gambitbooks.com

Edited by Graham Burgess
Typeset by Petra Nunn
All illustrations by Shane Mercer
Printed in the USA by Bang Printing, Brainerd, Minnesota

10 9 8 7 6 5 4 3 2 1

Gambit Publications Ltd
Directors: Dr John Nunn GM, Murray Chandler GM, and Graham Burgess FM
German Editor: Petra Nunn WFM

Contents

BUILDING A
BRIDGE

Chess Notation

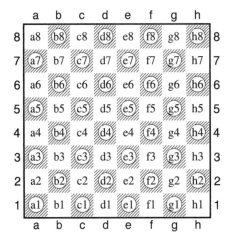

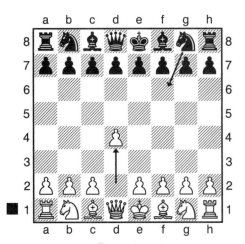

The chess moves in this book are written in the standard chess *notation* that is in use throughout the world. It can be learned by anyone in just a few minutes.

As you can see from the left-hand chessboard above, the vertical columns of squares (called *files*) are labelled a-h and the horizontal rows of squares (called *ranks*) are numbered 1-8. This gives each square its own unique name. The pieces are shown as follows:

Knight   =   ♘
Bishop   =   ♗
Rook   =   ♖
Queen   =   ♕
King   =   ♔

Pawns are not given a symbol. When they move, only the *destination square* is given.

In the right-hand diagram above, White has already played the move **1 d4**. The **1** indicates the move-number, and **d4** the destination square of the white pawn. Black is about to reply **1...♘f6** (moving his knight to the **f6-square** on his *first move*).

The following symbols are also used:
Check   =   +
Capture   =   x
Checkmate   =   #
Good move   =   !
Bad move   =   ?
Brilliant move   =   !!
Disastrous move =   ??

To check you've got the hang of it, play through the following moves on your chessboard: **1 e4 c6 2 ♘f3 d5 3 ♘c3 dxe4** (the pawn on the *d*-file captures on e4) **4 ♘xe4 ♘d7 5 ♕e2 ♘gf6??** (the knight on the *g*-file moves to f6 – this is a bad move!) **6 ♘d6#.** Checkmate! Black's pawn on e7 cannot take the knight as this would put his own king in check from the white queen.

Pawn promotion is written, for example, **d8♕**, meaning that a white pawn advances to d8 and becomes a queen.

Introduction

The endgame in chess arises when most of the pieces have disappeared from the board and only the kings, some pawns and a few other pieces are left. Not every game reaches an endgame, since some are decided in the middlegame or even the opening. However, in practice most games reach an endgame of one type or another. Just because there are few pieces left on the board does not mean that endgames are simpler than other parts of the game. On the contrary, since there is usually no comeback from a mistake in the endgame, accuracy is crucial.

This book aims to teach the reader how to play all the usual types of endgame. The chapters are organized according to the pieces on the board. If all the pieces have disappeared, so that only the kings and some pawns are left, that is a king and pawn ending, the subject of Chapter 2. Later chapters cover minor-piece endings, rook endings and so on. Each chapter starts with an explanation of four key themes in that type of ending, and then moves straight on to the exercises. Within each chapter, the exercises gradually increase in difficulty and, as some exercises build on earlier ones, it is best if they are tackled in sequence. It's advisable also to study the chapters in order, as some later chapters depend in a limited way on earlier chapters.

A small white or black square next to the diagram shows which player is to move. If there is both a white and a black square, then the position is considered both with White to move and with Black to move. Each exercise explains what you must do to solve it; for example, some ask you to find the best move, while others are multiple-choice questions. The exercises have been carefully chosen so that there is one clearly best solution, and all have been computer-checked for correctness. Each chapter ends with solutions which contain additional instructive comments. The final chapter is a series of test papers (with points awarded) featuring a mix of endgames. Don't be discouraged if you have problems solving some of the exercises, especially towards the end of the chapters. Once you have made a serious effort to solve a position, read the solution and learn everything you can from it. Then the next time you see the position or a similar one, you will find the key idea much more easily. There is little prior knowledge required for this book, other than the rules of chess and how the pieces move. A few common tactical ideas are mentioned, especially in Chapter 7. If in doubt about these, consult a book on basic tactics such as my own *Chess Tactics Workbook for Kids* (Gambit, 2019).

For some exercises it is helpful to know the usual result of certain endings without pawns. For convenience and easy reference I have gathered the information here:

Usual result of some endings without pawns			
K+Q vs K	Win	K+Q vs K+R	Win
K+R vs K	Win	K+R vs K+B	Draw
K+B+B vs K	Win	K+R vs K+N	Draw
K+B+N vs K	Win	K+R+B vs K+R	Draw
K+N+N vs K	Draw	K+R+N vs K+R	Draw

I hope that this book will help you to win games that reach an ending and to understand one of the most interesting parts of chess.

1 The Lone King

This first chapter deals with the case in which your opponent only has his king left and you need to deliver checkmate. There are four common winning situations, ♔+♕ vs ♚, ♔+♖ vs ♚, ♔+2♗ vs ♚ and ♔+♗+♘ vs ♚. In each case it is possible to force mate even against perfect defence. Surprisingly, it is not possible to force mate with king and two knights against a lone king. The first two cases are the most important since they occur so often in games.

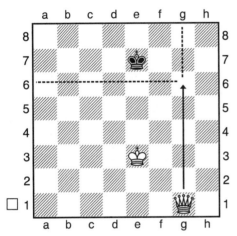

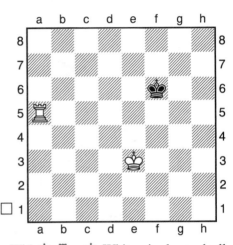

Here's a typical example of mating with ♔+♕ vs ♚. White can only deliver mate when the enemy king is on the edge of the board (this includes the corners). The key idea is to use the queen to confine the enemy king and this is usually done by **moves that do not give check**. Checking the king again and again is pointless as the queen cannot mate by itself; it needs the help of the king. **1 ♕g6!** (restricting the enemy king to the back two ranks) **1...♔d7** (Black tries to avoid having his king forced to the edge of the board) **2 ♔d4** (the king advances to help) **2...♔e7 3 ♔d5 ♔d7 4 ♕f7+** (the queen can give a check now that the white king is in position, since it forces Black's king to the edge of the board) **4...♔c8 5 ♔c6 ♔b8** (5...♔d8 can be met by 6 ♕f8# or 6 ♕d7#) **6 ♕b7#**.

With ♔+♖ vs ♚, White wins by gradually driving Black's king to the edge of the board and then into a corner. **1 ♔e4!** (1 ♔f4 is slower, as after 1...♔e6 White cannot immediately force the king back) **1...♔e6** (1...♔g6 2 ♖f5 creates a box confining the king to the top-right corner, after which White wins by 2...♔g7 3 ♔e5 ♔g6 4 ♔e6 ♔g7 5 ♖g5+ ♔h6 6 ♔f6 ♔h7 7 ♖g2 ♔h8 8 ♔f7 ♔h7 9 ♖h2#) **2 ♖a6+** (forcing the enemy king nearer the edge; 2 ♖d5 is another winning method based on creating a box for the enemy king) **2...♔e7 3 ♔d5** (Black tries to avoid having his king trapped on the edge of the board, but he cannot delay it for long) **3...♔f7** (3...♔d7 4 ♖a7+ leads to a quicker end) **4 ♔e5 ♔e7** (4...♔g7 5 ♖f6 is another box) **5 ♖a7+ ♔d8 6 ♔e6 ♔c8** (6...♔e8 7 ♖a8#) **7 ♔d6 ♔b8 8 ♖c7 ♔a8 9 ♔c6 ♔b8 10 ♔b6 ♔a8 11 ♖c8#**.

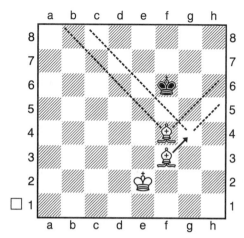

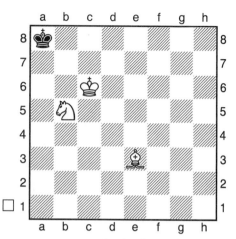

The idea of creating a barrier or box works just as well with ♔+2♗ vs ♚. **1 ♗g4** (this controls the h3-c8 diagonal so that the two bishops can confine the black king to the top-right corner) **1...♚g6 2 ♔e3** (once the enemy king is trapped in a box, White has unlimited time to bring his own king up to assist) **2...♚f6 3 ♔e4 ♚g6 4 ♔e5** (the king's influence starts to be felt and the area accessible to Black's king gradually shrinks) **4...♚f7** (now that ...♚f6 is impossible, White can nudge his bishops forwards without any fear of them being attacked by the enemy king) **5 ♗f5 ♚g7 6 ♔e6 ♚f8** (Black has no choice but to move to the edge of the board; now White must force the king into the corner) **7 ♔f6 ♚e8 8 ♗c7** (preventing the king from sneaking away via d8) **8...♚f8 9 ♗d7** (the two bishops cooperate perfectly to usher the king towards h8) **9...♚g8 10 ♔g6 ♚f8 11 ♗d6+** (now it just remains for the king to be checked to its doom) **11...♚g8 12 ♗e6+ ♚h8 13 ♗e5#**.

The mate with ♔+♗+♘ vs ♚ is *much* more advanced and we will only look at the final stages of the procedure. The difficulty is that mate can only be forced when the defending king is in one of the corners which can be controlled by the bishop, in this case a1 or h8. In the diagram, White plays to force the black king to h8. **1 ♘c7+ ♚b8 2 ♗f2** (waiting for ...♚c8 so that the king can be forced further along the eighth rank) **2...♚c8 3 ♗a7 ♚d8** (now White must stop the black king escaping via e7) **4 ♘d5 ♚e8 5 ♚d6 ♚f7** (threatening to slip away towards h1 via g6 and h5) **6 ♘e7!** (this is where players normally go wrong; the key idea is to put the knight on e7 so that a later ♗e3 will leave White controlling f5, g5, g6 and h6, setting up an impassable barrier to Black's king) **6...♚f6** (6...♚e8 7 ♚e6 ♚d8 8 ♗b6+ also herds the king towards h8, while 6...♚g7 7 ♗e3 ♚f6 8 ♗f4 is similar to the main line) **7 ♗e3! ♚f7 8 ♗g5** (further confining the king) **8...♚e8** (Black makes a last attempt to escape) **9 ♚e6** (the simplest win) **9...♚d8 10 ♗f4 ♚e8 11 ♗c7 ♚f8 12 ♘f5 ♚e8 13 ♘g7+ ♚f8 14 ♚f6 ♚g8 15 ♚g6 ♚f8 16 ♗d6+ ♚g8 17 ♗e7** (a waiting move) **17...♚h8 18 ♘f5 ♚g8 19 ♘h6+ ♚h8 20 ♗f6#**.

Exercises

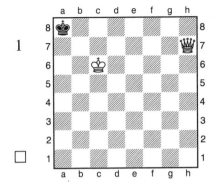

1

How can White mate in one move?

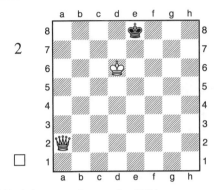

2

Find the mate in one for White.

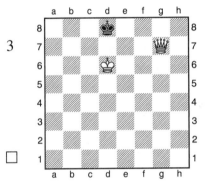

3

How many ways can White mate in one?

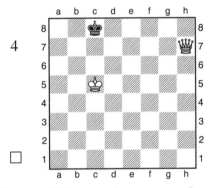

4

How can White mate in two moves?

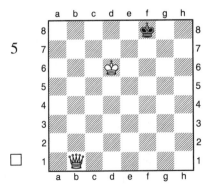

5

Which move leads to mate in two?

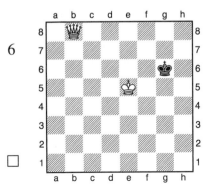

6

How does White force mate in three moves?

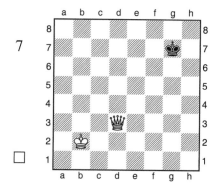

7

Which move puts the enemy king in a small box and leads to the quickest mate?

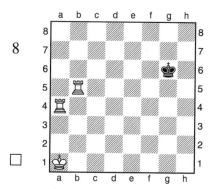

8

How can White mate in three moves?

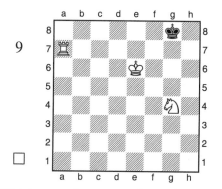

9

Which move forces mate in two?

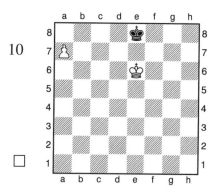

10

How many ways can White mate in one?

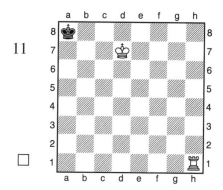

11

Find the only move to mate in two.

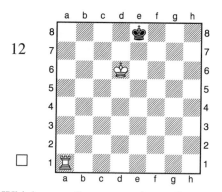

12

Which move forces mate in two?

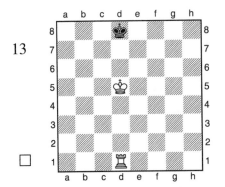

13

How can White force mate in three moves?

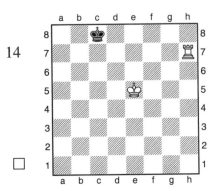

14

How does White mate in four moves?

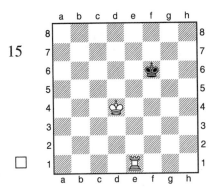

15

Which move creates a box around the black king?

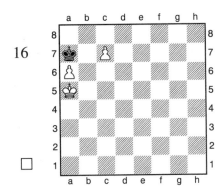

16

How can White mate in three?

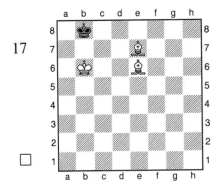

17

How does White mate in two?

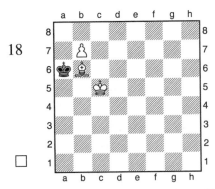

18

Which is the only move to win for White?

Tougher Exercises

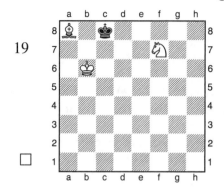

19

Why is 1 ♘d6+?? a blunder?

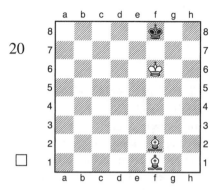

20

Which move prevents the black king from escaping and so forces mate in five moves?

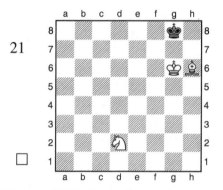

21

How can White force mate in three moves?

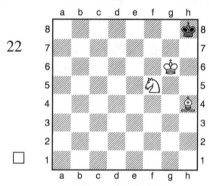

22

How does White force mate in three moves here?

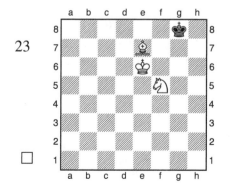

23

Using the finish of the previous exercise, can you see how White can force mate in five moves?

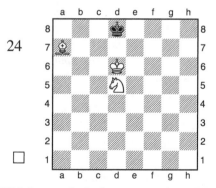

24

Which move is the best way to force Black's king towards the h8-corner?

Solutions to The Lone King Exercises

1) 1 Qb7#.

2) 1 Qg8#.

3) There are four possible mates in one: **1 Qd7#, 1 Qf8#, 1 Qg8#** and **1 Qh8#**.

4) White mates in two by closing in with his king: **1 Kc6 Kd8** (or 1...Kb8 2 Qb7#) **2 Qd7#**.

5) **1 Qh7!** (not 1 Qg6??, stalemating Black) **1...Ke8 2 Qg8#** (or 2 Qe7#). Notice that to win you often need to play moves that aren't checks. Just checking repeatedly will only drive the enemy king in circles.

6) Mating with king and queen involves using both pieces in combination to drive the enemy king to the edge of the board. Here this can be done by **1 Qg8+ Kh5 2 Kf5 Kh4** (2...Kh6 is met by 3 Qh8# or 3 Qg6#) **3 Qg4#**.

7) **1 Qf5!** confines the black king to the four squares g7, g8, h6 and h8, allowing White to bring his own king up to finish Black off. You just need to make sure the enemy king has at least one move, as otherwise it is stalemate! The end might be **1...Kg8** (1...Kh6 2 Qg4 followed by playing the king to f6 is basically the same) **2 Qd7** (it's easy to mate when the enemy king is confined to the back rank) **2...Kf8 3 Kc3 Kg8 4 Kd4 Kf8 5 Ke5 Kg8 6 Kf6 Kh8** (or 6...Kf8 7 Qf7#) **7 Qg7#**.

8) **1 Ra6+ Kf7 2 Rb7+ Ke8 3 Ra8#.** This 'lawnmower mate' is a good way to finish the game if you have a lot of extra material. It also works if you have a queen and a rook.

9) White could win with just his rook, but the extra knight makes it easier: **1 Nf6+! Kf8** (or 1...Kh8 2 Rh7#) **2 Rf7#**.

10) There are two possible mates in one: **1 a8Q#** or **1 a8R#**, the latter being an *underpromotion*.

11) White's king and rook work together to mate by **1 Kc7 Ka7 2 Ra1#**.

12) After **1 Rf1!** there is no threat, but Black has only one legal move, **1...Kd8**, which allows **2 Rf8#**.

13) **1 Kd6!** (this confines the black king and leaves it with only two possible moves) **1...Kc8** (1...Ke8 2 Rf1 is a mirror image) **2 Rb1** (this is the key move: White has no threat, but Black must make a move and is obliged to walk into a mate) **2...Kd8** (mate is possible when the kings face each other with the enemy king on the edge of the board) **3 Rb8#**.

14) With K+R vs K, the final stage arises when the enemy king is trapped on the back rank. After **1 Kd6** Black must move his king somewhere, and since 1...Kd8 2 Rh8# is immediate mate, he has no choice but to move to b8. However, after **1...Kb8 2 Kc6** it's the same again. 2...Kc8 allows 3 Rh8# so the king is driven into the corner and is finished off by **2...Ka8 3 Kb6 Kb8 4 Rh8#**.

15) **1 Re5!** traps the king in the top right corner of the board. It's worth seeing how White gradually drives the enemy king to the edge of the board, when he wins as in Exercise 14. **1...Kf7 2 Kd5 Kf6 3 Kd6 Kf7 4 Rf5+ Kg6** (the box gradually grows smaller as the king is driven towards the edge of the board; 4...Kg7 5 Ke6 Kg6 6 Ra5 is similar) **5 Ke6 Kg7 6 Rg5+** (now the king must move to the edge) **6...Kh6** (or 6...Kf8 7 Rg1 Ke8 8 Rg8#) **7 Kf6 Kh7 8 Rg1** (now it's the mate of the previous exercise) **8...Kh8 9 Kf7 Kh7 10 Rh1#**.

16) 1 ♔b5! (1 c8♕? and 1 c8♖? both stalemate Black) **1...♚a8 2 c8♕+** (now it's safe to promote) **2...♚a7 3 ♕b7#**.

17) 1 ♗d6+ ♚a8 2 ♗d5#.

18) **1 b8♘+!** wins as king, bishop and knight beat a lone king. Instead 1 ♔c6?, 1 b8♕? and 1 b8♖? all stalemate Black, while after 1 b8♗? White has two bishops, but they both move on dark squares so mate is impossible.

19) 1 ♘d6+?? is a blunder because after 1...♚b8! White can only save his bishop by moving it along the diagonal, but then Black is stalemated. Instead, White can force mate most easily by **1 ♗c6 ♚b8 2 ♗d7 ♚a8** (now White only needs to play his knight to a6) **3 ♘e5 ♚b8 4 ♘c6+ ♚a8 5 ♔b4 ♚b8 6 ♘a6+ ♚a8 7 ♗c6#**.

20) In order to mate with two bishops, you must drive the enemy king into a corner. Here the nearest corner is h8, so the first step is to prevent the king from escaping via e8. **1 ♗b5! ♚g8 2 ♔g6 ♚f8** (or 2...♚h8 3 ♗c5 ♚g8 4 ♗c4+ ♚h8 5 ♗d4#) **3 ♗c5+ ♚g8 4 ♗c4+ ♚h8 5 ♗d4#**. The final moves here are the diagonal equivalent of the 'lawnmower' mate from Exercise 8. The two bishops operate on parallel diagonals to chase the enemy king to its doom.

21) It's possible to mate with ♗+♘ against a lone king, but it's not easy because you must chase the enemy king into one of the two corners where the corner square can be controlled by the bishop. This example shows the final stage once the enemy king is in the correct corner. **1 ♘e4! ♚h8 2 ♗g7+** (not 2 ♘f6?? stalemate) **2...♚g8 3 ♘f6#**.

22) **1 ♗e7!** stops the enemy king from escaping to f8 on the next move and mates after **1...♚g8 2 ♘h6+ ♚h8 3 ♗f6#**. This time it's the bishop that gives the mate rather than the knight. Once the enemy king is in the correct corner, there's normally a choice of mates and it doesn't matter which one you play.

23) All three pieces must work together to finish Black off. First the white king moves to g6, restricting the enemy king to the squares g8 and h8. Remember that you must leave a square for Black's king, as otherwise it will be stalemate. **1 ♔f6! ♚h7** (1...♚h8 2 ♔g6 ♚g8 3 ♘h6+ ♚h8 4 ♗f6# mates one move more quickly) **2 ♔f7 ♚h8 3 ♔g6 ♚g8 4 ♘h6+ ♚h8 5 ♗f6#**.

24) The best move is **1 ♘e7!**, which stops the king from moving to c8, so it must go the other way, towards h8. 1 ♘b6? also covers c8 but blocks the bishop in and so makes the win more difficult. The finish might be **1...♚e8** (now Black threatens to escape via f7 and f6, so White hurries to prevent that using his own king) **2 ♔e6 ♚d8** (Black is putting up a good fight and now intends to slip out via c7) **3 ♗b6+** (the bishop jumps in to stop ...♚c7; notice how White must use all three pieces together to stop the enemy king from escaping the back rank) **3...♚e8 4 ♘f5** (we saw in the previous exercise that this is a good square for the knight in the final mate) **4...♚f8 5 ♗d4** (the bishop is heading for f6) **5...♚e8** (or 5...♚g8 6 ♗c5 ♚h8 7 ♔f6 ♚g8 8 ♔g6 ♚h8 and now White just has to wait with his bishop to get the mate of the previous exercise: 9 ♗d6 ♚g8 10 ♘h6+ ♚h8 11 ♗e5#) **6 ♗f6** (stopping the king from escaping via d8 and being ready to check on e7) **6...♚f8 7 ♗e7+ ♚g8** (7...♚e8 8 ♘d6#) and now we have the position of the previous exercise, with the finish **8 ♔f6 ♚h7 9 ♔f7 ♚h8 10 ♔g6 ♚g8 11 ♘h6+ ♚h8 12 ♗f6#**.

13

2 King and Pawn Endings

The most basic type of ending is that with only the kings and some pawns. Any other ending can lead to a king and pawn ending after an exchange of pieces, so understanding this ending is the basis for almost all endgame knowledge.

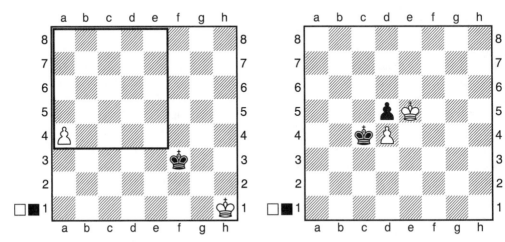

A *passed pawn* is one that can advance to the eighth rank without being blocked or captured by an enemy pawn. Passed pawns are very important in king and pawn endings because only the king can stop them. In the diagram, the result depends on who is to play. If White moves first, **1 a5 ♔e4 2 a6 ♔d5 3 a7 ♔c6 4 a8♕+** wins (see ♔+♕ vs ♔ in Chapter 1). However, if it is Black's move, he catches the pawn by **1...♔e4 2 a5 ♔d5 3 a6 ♔c6 4 a7 ♔b7** and the result is a draw.

To work out whether the pawn can be caught, it may help to visualize a square, as indicated on the diagram, with one side joining the promotion square to the square occupied by the pawn. If Black can enter this square with his king, then he will catch the pawn. One warning: when the pawn is on the second rank, the square must be drawn back to the third rank rather than the second, due to the initial double move of the pawn.

A key concept in endings generally, but especially in king and pawn endings, is that of *zugzwang*. This odd-looking German word (pronounced *tsugtsvang*) has no real English equivalent and is universally used in the chess world. Zugzwang occurs when every legal move harms your position. You would prefer not to make a move at all and just pass, but the laws of chess forbid this.

In the diagram, suppose that it is White to play. His king is currently defending his last pawn, but any move leaves the pawn undefended and allows Black to take it. We say that White is in zugzwang. After **1 ♔f4 ♔xd4 2 ♔f3 ♔d3 3 ♔f2 ♔d2** there is nothing White can do to prevent ...d4, ...d3, ...♔c2, ...d2 and ...d1♕, promoting the pawn and winning. If Black is to play, he must leave the d5-pawn unguarded, allowing White to take it and win in a similar way, so *whoever moves first loses*.

14

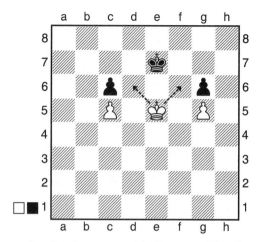

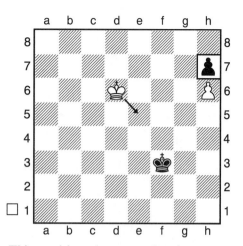

Another key concept is the *opposition*. In the diagram, White would like to move his king to d6 or f6, winning a pawn and the game, but right now Black's king is guarding both squares. If it is Black to play, then he must move his king one way or the other, allowing the white king in. In this case we say that White has the opposition. Play may continue **1...♔d7 2 ♔f6 ♔d8 3 ♔xg6 ♔e7 4 ♔h7** and White promotes his g-pawn, or the mirror-image line **1...♔f7 2 ♔d6 ♔e8 3 ♔xc6 ♔e7 4 ♔b7**, also with an easy win for White. If it is White to play, then the position is a draw. He should not play 1 ♔e4? ♔e6, when it is Black who has the opposition and wins. Instead, White should play **1 ♔d4!** (1 ♔f4! ♔e6 2 ♔e4 is just as good) **1...♔e6 2 ♔e4**, which avoids giving Black the opposition. Then after **2...♔d7!** (but not 2...♔e7? 3 ♔e5) **3 ♔e5 ♔e7** the diagram position is repeated and the result will be a draw. The key feature here is the way the kings oppose each other (hence the name 'opposition') with one empty square in between. If there are no spare pawn moves, then whoever moves first must allow the enemy king to advance. This is a situation of zugzwang, but it occurs so often that it deserves its own name.

This position shows another important idea, called *shouldering away*, which involves using your own king to deny squares to the enemy king. In the diagram, if White is to play he can head for the h7-pawn and take it, but does this win the game? Let's try **1 ♔e6** and see what happens. Play continues **1...♔e4 2 ♔f6 ♔d5 3 ♔g7 ♔e6 4 ♔xh7 ♔f7 5 ♔h8 ♔f8**. This position is a draw because the white king is blocking his own pawn, so he can only repeat by **6 ♔h7 ♔f7** or get himself stalemated after **6 h7 ♔f7**. So how does White win? It was the very first move that was wrong, since instead of 1 ♔e6? White should have played **1 ♔e5!**. This also leads to the capture of the h7-pawn, but without allowing the black king to reach f7 and confine the white king to the h-file. White then wins after **1...♔e3 2 ♔f6 ♔f4 3 ♔g7 ♔g5 4 ♔xh7 ♔f6 5 ♔g8** or **1...♔g4 2 ♔f6 ♔h5 3 ♔g7 ♔g5 4 ♔xh7 ♔f6 5 ♔g8** followed by promoting the h-pawn in either case. This works because the routes d6-e6-f6-g7-h7 and d6-e5-f6-g7-h7 both take the same length of time, four moves, but the latter route also keeps the black king at arm's length and prevents it from moving to e4 or f4 on the first move.

15

Exercises

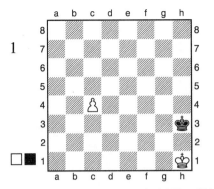

1

If White is to play, can he win? What if it is Black to play?

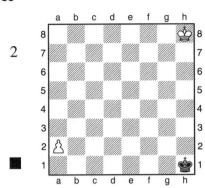

2

Can Black (to play) draw?

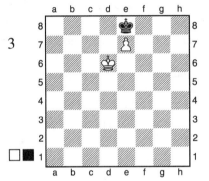

3

Can White win if it is his move? And if it is Black to play?

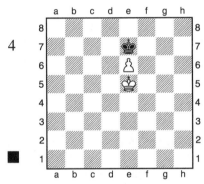

4

What should Black play: 1...♔f8, 1...♔e8 or 1...♔d8, or do all of them draw?

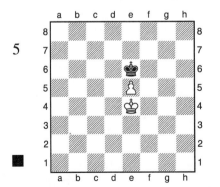

5

Which is correct: 1...♔f7, 1...♔e7 or 1...♔d7, or do all of them draw?

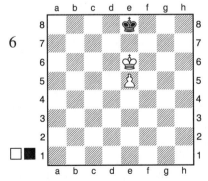

6

Is this a win with Black to play? How about if White is to play?

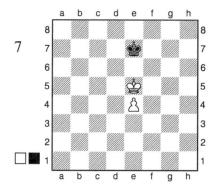

7

Can White win if Black is to play? How about if White is to play?

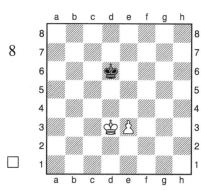

8

Which is the best move: 1 e4, 1 ♔d4 or 1 ♔e4?

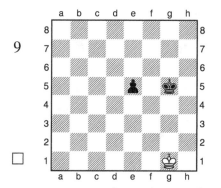

9

Should White play 1 ♔f1, 1 ♔f2 or 1 ♔g2?

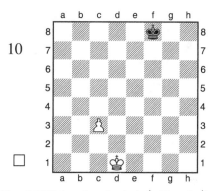

10

Should White play 1 c4, 1 ♔d2 or 1 ♔c2?

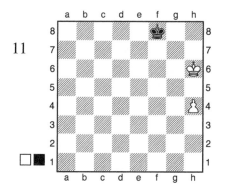

11

Is this a win with Black to play? How about with White to play?

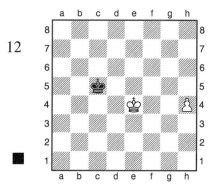

12

Can Black (to play) draw?

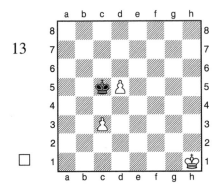

13

Can White (to play) win?

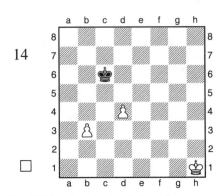

14

Can White (to play) win here?

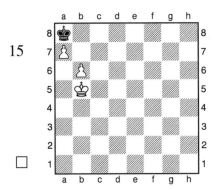

15

1 ♔c6 and 1 ♔a6 give stalemate, so is it possible for White to win?

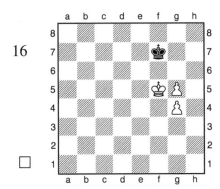

16

Can White win this position?

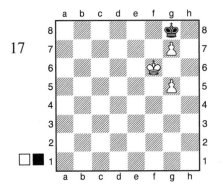

17

If White is to play, can he win? What about if Black is to play?

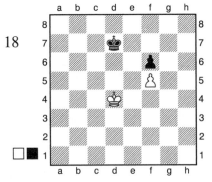

18

What is the result if White moves first? And if Black moves first?

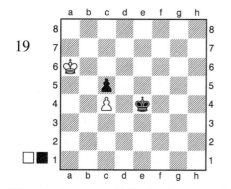

19

What is the result if White is to play? If Black is to play?

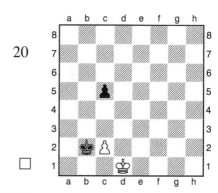

20

Which move secures the draw: 1 c3, 1 c4 or 1 ♔d2?

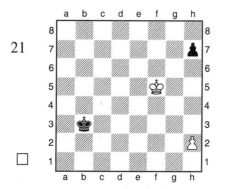

21

Is the winning move 1 ♔f6, 1 ♔g5 or 1 h4?

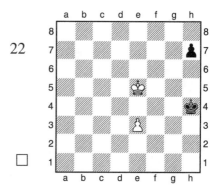

22

Which move is best: 1 ♔f4, 1 ♔f5 or 1 e4?

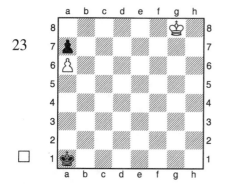

23

The win looks simple, but White must take care. What should he play?

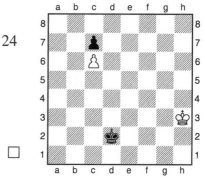

24

What should White play: 1 ♔g2, 1 ♔g3 or 1 ♔g4?

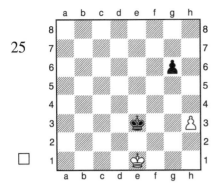

25

How does White draw?

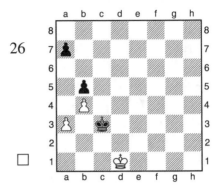

26

Can White save the game?

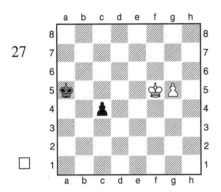

27

Is it possible for White to win?

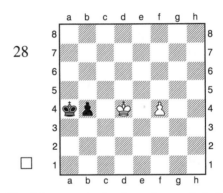

28

Black's pawn is further advanced, but despite this White can win. How?

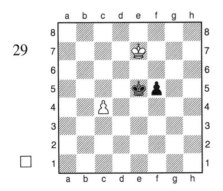

29

How can White draw?

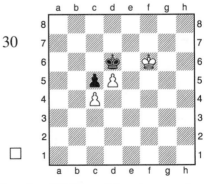

30

How does White use his extra pawn to win?

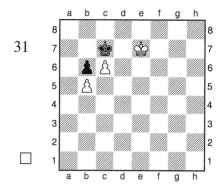

31

This is also a win, but how?

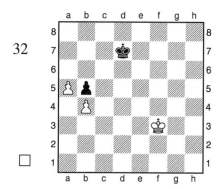

32

Can White win in this position?

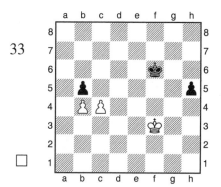

33

Which is correct: 1 cxb5 or 1 c5?

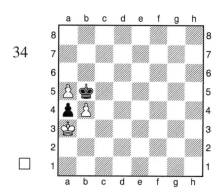

34

How does White win this?

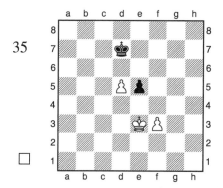

35

What should White play, 1 ♔d3 or 1 ♔e4, and how does he follow it up?

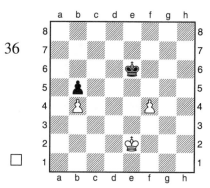

36

Can White win this position?

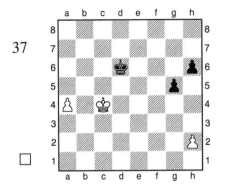

37

Material is equal. Who has the advantage and why?

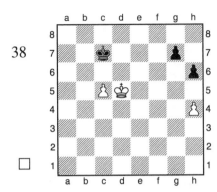

38

What's the best move for White: 1 c6, 1 h5 or 1 ♔e6?

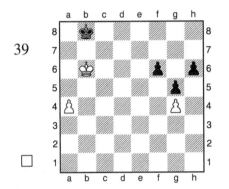

39

Should White play 1 a5 or 1 ♔c6, and what is the result?

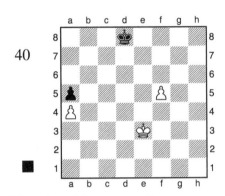

40

What should the result be?

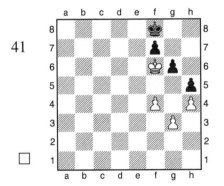

41

Does White have to be satisfied with a draw?

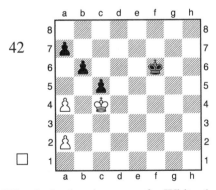

42

What is the drawing move for White: 1 a5, 1 ♔b5 or 1 ♔d5?

Tougher Exercises

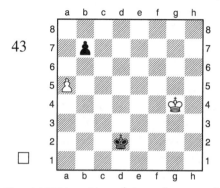

43

Should White play 1 ♔f3, 1 ♔f4 or 1 ♔f5?

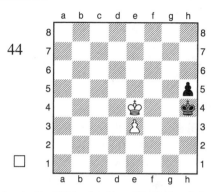

44

A win for White looks unlikely, but it is possible. How?

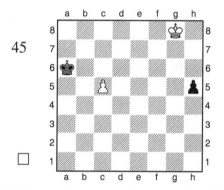

45

White can draw using a cunning idea. What is it?

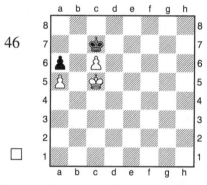

46

Exercise 34 might help you work out how White can win here.

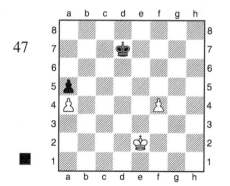

47

This is similar to Exercise 40, but the pawn is on f4 instead of f5. Can Black (to play) draw here?

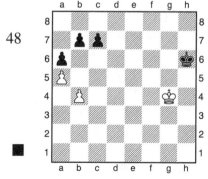

48

Which is correct: 1...♔g6 or 1...b6?

Solutions to King and Pawn Endings Exercises

1) If White is to play, he wins as Black's king cannot catch the pawn: **1 c5 ♚g4 2 c6 ♚f5 3 c7 ♚e6 4 c8♕+**. With Black to play, the extra move means that he can stop the pawn and draw: **1...♚g4 2 c5 ♚f5 3 c6 ♚e6 4 c7 ♚d7**.

2) It's a win for White even with Black to play since the pawn cannot be caught: **1...♚g2 2 a4 ♚f3 3 a5 ♚e4 4 a6 ♚d5 5 a7 ♚c6 6 a8♕+**. The initial double move of White's pawn acted as a booster to propel it beyond the range of Black's king.

3) With White to play, he cannot win as the only move to keep the pawn, **1 ♚e6**, stalemates Black. If it is Black to play then his only move is **1...♚f7** but after **2 ♚d7** White can promote his pawn. This is another position of zugzwang (see the chapter introduction on page 14) in which whoever moves first must damage his own position.

4) 1...♚d8? 2 ♚d6 ♚e8 3 e7 ♚f7 4 ♚d7 and 1...♚f8? 2 ♚f6 ♚e8 3 e7 ♚d7 4 ♚f7 are both losing for Black. In this position, moving straight backwards is correct and **1...♚e8!** is the only move to draw. Then **2 ♚d6** (2 ♚f6 ♚f8 is just a mirror image) **2...♚d8 3 e7+ ♚e8** leads to Exercise 3, where the only move to keep the pawn, **4 ♚e6**, stalemates Black.

5) All three moves draw. Not only does **1...♚e7 2 ♚d5 ♚d7 3 e6+ ♚e7 4 ♚e5 ♚e8!** draw (see Exercise 4), but also **1...♚d7** (1...♚f7 draws the same way) **2 ♚d5 ♚e7 3 e6 ♚e8!** draws, since it doesn't matter whether White's king is on d5 or e5. You only need to be careful about where you retreat your king when the pawn is on the sixth rank, but to avoid confusion most players move their king straight backwards whichever rank the pawn is on.

6) It's a win whoever moves first. With Black to play, after **1...♚d8 2 ♚f7** or **1...♚f8 2 ♚d7** the pawn advances to the eighth rank. If White is to play, he wins by **1 ♚d6** (1 ♚f6 is just as good) **1...♚d8 2 e6 ♚e8 3 e7 ♚f7 4 ♚d7**, as in Exercise 3 with Black to play. This position is important precisely because it's a win whoever moves first, so you don't need to worry about which player is to move.

7) The result is different when the pawn is further back and here the result depends on who is to move. If Black is to play, he must allow the white king to advance, and then White wins: **1...♚f7** (1...♚d7 2 ♚f6 is a mirror image) **2 ♚d6 ♚e8 3 e5 ♚d8 4 e6 ♚e8 5 e7** and the pawn will promote. However, it's a draw with White to play since Black can keep the king out: **1 ♚d5 ♚d7 2 e5 ♚e7 3 e6 ♚e8!**, as in Exercise 4. This position is an example of the opposition (see the chapter introduction on page 15).

8) 1 e4? ♚e5 is drawn as in Exercise 5, while after 1 ♚e4? ♚e6 2 ♚f4 ♚f6 Black has the opposition and can prevent the white king from advancing, similar to Exercise 7 with White to play. **1 ♚d4!** is the only move to win, gaining the opposition. After **1...♚e6 2 ♚e4** the king advances; for example, **2...♚d6 3 ♚f5 ♚e7 4 ♚e5 ♚d7 5 ♚f6** followed by pushing the e-pawn. The general principle here is that it is generally **better for the attacker to have his king in front of his pawn**.

9) 1 ♚f2? ♚f4 2 ♚e2 ♚e4 and 1 ♚g2? ♚g4! 2 ♚f2 ♚f3 3 ♚e2 ♚e4 both lead to Exercise 7 (with colours reversed). In both lines White is to play, so Black has the opposition and wins. Surprisingly, **1 ♚f1!** is the only move to draw. Then **1...♚f5** (the trickiest reply; after 1...♚f4 2 ♚f2 ♚e4 3 ♚e2 White gains the opposition and draws) **2 ♚e1!** (2 ♚e2? ♚e4 and 2 ♚f2? ♚f4 3 ♚e2 ♚e4 are both wrong) **2...♚f4** (or 2...♚e4 3 ♚e2; note that 2...♚e5 would maintain the opposition, but Black's pawn is blocking that square) **3 ♔f2! ♚e4 4 ♔e2** is a draw by Exercise 7 as now Black is to play and so it is White who has the opposition.

10) 1 ♔d2? ♚e7 2 ♔d3 ♚d7! draws after 3 ♔d4 ♚d6 or 3 ♔c4 ♚c6, as in the previous exercise, while 1 c4? ♚e7 2 ♔c2 ♚d6 is an easy draw. **1 ♔c2!** is the way to win, since after **1...♚e7 2 ♔b3 ♚d6 3 ♔b4!** (not 3 ♔c4? ♚c6) **3...♚c6** (3...♚d5 4 ♔b5 is also winning for White) **4 ♔c4!** White gains the opposition and wins as in Exercise 8.

11) It's a draw whoever moves first. Rook's pawns are a special case and many positions are drawn because the edge of the board creates additional stalemate possibilities. If Black is to play, he draws by **1...♚g8 2 h5 ♚h8 3 ♚g6 ♚g8 4 h6 ♚h8** and now **5 h7** is stalemate as there is no 'i7' square! If White is to play, he fares no better: **1 ♔h7 ♚f7 2 h5 ♚f8 3 h6** (or 3 ♔g6 ♚g8 4 h6 ♚h8 5 h7 as before) **3...♚f7 4 ♔h8 ♚f8 5 h7 ♚f7** and now White is stalemated.

12) Black draws by **1...♚d6! 2 ♔f5** (or 2 h5 ♚e7 3 h6 ♚f8 and the pawn is stopped) **2...♚e7 3 ♔g6 ♚f8**, leading to the previous exercise. The basic rule is that if Black's king reaches f8 without allowing an immediate promotion, then the game will be a draw.

13) 1 c4! wins for White, as Black cannot play 1...♚xc4 due to 2 d6, when the d-pawn promotes. This means that the pawns are invulnerable, and White has all the time in the world to bring his king up to support the pawns: **1...♚d6 2 ♔g2 ♚c5 3 ♔f3 ♚d6 4 ♔e4 ♚d7 5 c5** and the pawns advance, with an easy win.

14) Black threatens to win both pawns by ...♚d5, and **1 b4!** is the only way to meet this threat. Now White wins, as the pawns support each other: **1...♚b5** (1...♚d5 2 b5 is essentially the same) **2 d5 ♚b6** (2...♚xb4 3 d6) **3 ♔g2 ♚c7** (threatening 4...♚d6) **4 b5** and the pawns support each other again. If White is careful, Black can never take one of the pawns, so White can win by using his king to assist the pawns.

15) White can win, but it is quite tricky: **1 ♔c5 ♚b7 2 a8♕+!** (surprisingly, the only way to win is to give up one of the pawns, thereby allowing the king to advance without giving stalemate) **2...♚xa8 3 ♔c6 ♚b8 4 b7 ♚a7 5 ♔c7** and the remaining pawn promotes.

16) White wins with doubled pawns because he can use the rear pawn to lose time: **1 g6+ ♚g7 2 ♔g5 ♚g8 3 ♚h6** (3 ♔f6 also wins, but is more complicated) **3...♚h8 4 g7+ ♚g8** (this is where the second pawn comes in handy) **5 g5 ♚f7 6 ♚h7** and the front pawn promotes.

17) Problems can arise with doubled pawns if one of them has been advanced to the seventh rank without thinking ahead. Here if White is to play he can only draw as **1 g6** and **1 ♔g6** are stalemate, while otherwise White must give up the g7-pawn, leading to the draw of Exercise 4. If Black is to move then White wins, but he must give up the front pawn to succeed: **1...♚h7 2 g8♕+!** (2 g6+? ♚g8 and 2 ♔f7? only draw, the latter due to immediate stalemate) **2...♚xg8 3 ♔g6** with the win of Exercise 6.

18) If White is to move, he wins the f6-pawn and the game by **1 ♔d5!**, gaining the opposition; for example, **1...♚e7 2 ♔c6 ♚e8 3 ♔d6 ♚f7 4 ♔d7 ♚f8 5 ♔e6 ♚g7 6 ♔e7 ♚g8 7 ♔xf6 ♚f8** with Exercise 6. If it is Black to play, he can win the f5-pawn but not the game: **1...♚d6 2 ♔e4 ♚c5 3 ♔e3 ♚d5 4 ♔f4 ♚d4 5 ♔f3 ♚e5 6 ♔g4 ♚e4 7 ♔g3 ♚xf5 8 ♔f3**. It may seem odd that White wins when he has the opposition while Black only draws when he has it. The reason is that White's pawn is further advanced, so White can reach the winning Exercise 6, while Black can only reach the drawing Exercise 7.

19) When White is to play, he wins by **1 ♔b6!** (not 1 ♔b5?? ♚d4, when it is Black who wins) **1...♚d4** (the only move to defend the pawn) **2 ♔b5** and White not only wins the enemy pawn, but with his king in front of his own pawn he also wins the game (see the second diagram on page 14). If Black moves first, he can win the same way by **1...♔d3! 2 ♚b5 ♔d4**.

20) 1 c3? ♔xc3 2 ♚c1 c4 is the win of Exercise 6, while 1 ♔d2? c4 2 c3 ♚b3 3 ♔d1 ♚xc3 4 ♔c1 leads to the same diagram with the other player to move. This emphasizes the importance of Exercise 6, as the win does not depend on whose move it is. **1 c4!** is the only way to draw since after **1...♔c3 2 ♚c1 ♔xc4 3 ♚c2** White has the opposition, and so draws as in Exercise 7.

21) 1 ♔f6? ♚c4 2 ♔g7 h5! 3 h4 ♚d5 4 ♔g6 ♚e6 5 ♔xh5 ♚f7 and 1 h4? ♚c4 2 h5 ♚d5 3 ♔f6 ♚d6 4 ♔g7 ♚e7 5 ♔xh7 ♚f8 are only draws. The win is **1 ♔g5!** (this enables White to take on h7 while preventing Black's king from reaching the drawing square f8) **1...♚c4 2 ♔h6 ♚d5 3 ♔xh7 ♚e6 4 ♔g6!** (after 4 ♔g7? ♚f5 5 h4 ♚g4 White loses the pawn) **4...♚e7 5 ♔g7 ♚e6 6 h4 ♚f5 7 h5** and the pawn will promote.

22) The 'shouldering away' idea, which involves using your own king to block the opponent's, is a key endgame concept (see the second diagram on page 15). Here White wins by using this idea several times: **1 ♔f4!** (1 ♔f5? ♚g3 2 e4 h5 leads to a draw, as does 1 e4? ♚g5) **1...♚h5 2 ♔f5! ♚h6 3 ♔f6!** (now Black must waste time) **3...♚h5 4 e4 ♚g4 5 e5 h5 6 e6 h4 7 e7 h3 8 e8♕ h2 9 ♕e4+** and White wins.

23) White must play ♔xa7 without allowing the drawing reply ...♚c7. To achieve this, he must shoulder away Black's king and block its path to c7: **1 ♔f7! ♚b2 2 ♔e6! ♚c3 3 ♔d5!** (3 ♔d6? shows why the king has to reach a7 via d5, as now 3...♚d4 4 ♔c6 ♚e5 5 ♔b7 ♚d6 6 ♔xa7 ♚c7 leads to a draw) **3...♚d3** (Black loses because he cannot now reach c7 in time) **4 ♔c6 ♚c4 5 ♔b7 ♚b5 6 ♔xa7 ♚c6 7 ♔b8** and White wins.

24) In order to draw, White must be able to meet ...♚xc6 with ♔c4, gaining the opposition (see Exercise 7). Black is going to make this hard by using his king to block the route to c4. Black wins after 1 ♔g3? ♚e3! 2 ♔g2 ♚d4 3 ♔f3 ♚d5 4 ♔e3 ♚xc6 as White is too far away to play ♔c4, while 1 ♔g4? ♚e3 2 ♔f5 ♚d4 3 ♔e6 ♚c5 4 ♔d7 ♚b6 puts White in zugzwang. The saving line is **1 ♔g2!** (the only way around the enemy king is via f1) **1...♚e2** (Black tries to shoulder away the white king and prevent it from moving to f1; 1...♚e3 2 ♔f1 transposes) **2 ♔g1!** (2 ♔g3? ♚e3! wins for Black as after 1 ♔g3?) **2...♚e3 3 ♔f1 ♚d4 4 ♔e2 ♚c5 5 ♔d3 ♚xc6 6 ♔c4** and White makes it to c4, drawing.

25) 1 ♔f1? ♚f3 2 h4 ♚g4 3 ♔g2 ♚xh4 4 ♔h2 ♚g4 5 ♔g2 g5 wins for Black as in Exercise 7, since he has the opposition. The key idea is to convert Black's g-pawn into an h-pawn, since rook's pawns allow far more drawing chances than other pawns. White's pawn is doomed in any case, so he may as well use it to devalue Black's pawn. **1 h4! ♔f3 2 h5! gxh5 3 ♔f1 ♚g3 4 ♔g1** leads to a draw as in Exercise 11.

26) White's position looks hopeless, as Black is threatening to take both white pawns, but White can draw provided he remembers that rook's pawns don't offer many winning chances. **1 a4!** (not 1 ♔c1? ♚b3, when White loses both pawns, but now Black will end up with only rook's pawns, and two are no better than one) **1...bxa4** (1...a6 2 axb5 axb5 3 ♔c1 ♚xb4 4 ♔b2 is a draw by Exercise 7) **2 ♔c1 a3 3 ♔b1** (stopping the a3-pawn)

3...♔xb4 4 ♔a2 and it's a draw as in Exercise 11, as the extra black pawn makes no difference at all.

27) If both sides promote, the game will be a draw, but White can win by forcing Black to put his king where White will promote with check. **1 ♔e4!** (1 g6? c3 2 g7 c2 3 g8♕ c1♕ is a draw) **1...♔b4** (1...c3 2 ♔d3 ♔b4 loses after 3 ♔c2 or 3 g6) **2 g6 c3 3 ♔d3! ♔b3** (otherwise Black cannot advance his pawn) **4 g7 c2 5 g8♕+** and White wins. The 'promotion with check' idea is often used to win pawn races that look as if they are going to end in a tie.

28) **1 f5 b3 2 ♔c3!** (a similar manoeuvre to the previous exercise, but this time it is combined with a second idea) **2...♔a3 3 f6 b2 4 f7 b1♕** (Black promotes first, but amazingly still loses) **5 f8♕+ ♔a4** (or 5...♔a2 6 ♕a8#) **6 ♕a8+** (if both sides promote then the result is generally a draw, but in this special case White can win with a tactic) **6...♔b5 7 ♕b8+** and the skewer wins Black's queen.

29) Black's pawn apparently can't be stopped, but White can achieve the seemingly impossible by a tricky king manoeuvre: **1 ♔d7!** (1 c5? ♔d5 is hopeless for White) **1...♔d4** (or 1...f4 2 c5 f3 3 c6 f2 4 c7 f1♕ 5 c8♕ with a draw) **2 ♔d6!** (White uses his king to do two things at the same time: he threatens to push his own pawn, and he also moves closer to Black's pawn) **2...♔xc4** (2...f4 3 c5 is a draw as before) **3 ♔e5** and the black pawn has been caught.

30) A passed pawn which is defended by another pawn, such as the d5-pawn here, is called a *protected passed pawn*. In pawn endings, having a protected passed pawn is usually a large advantage and, other things being equal, may well be enough to win all by itself. Here White wins by **1 ♔f5!** (after 1 ♔f7 ♔d7 2 ♔f8 ♔d8 White hasn't made progress) **1...♔e7 2 ♔e5 ♔d7 3 d6 ♔d8 4 ♔d5**, picking up Black's last pawn.

31) It's slightly trickier when the protected passed pawn is on the sixth rank. **1 ♔e6 ♔c8 2 c7!** (sacrificing the pawn is the only way to win; the method of Exercise 30 doesn't work here since 2 ♔d6 ♔d8 3 c7+ ♔c8 4 ♔c6? is stalemate, although White can still win in this line by going into reverse with 4 ♔e6!) **2...♔xc7 3 ♔e7 ♔c8 4 ♔d6** and White will win as in Exercise 18; for example, **4...♔b7 5 ♔d7 ♔b8 6 ♔c6 ♔a7 7 ♔c7 ♔a8 8 ♔xb6 ♔b8 9 ♔a6 ♔a8 10 b6 ♔b8 11 b7 ♔c7 12 ♔a7**.

32) White wins because the black king cannot move to the e-file, since then the a-pawn would promote. This means that Black cannot keep the white king out: **1 ♔e4 ♔d6** (1...♔e6 2 a6) **2 ♔d4 ♔c6 3 ♔e5 ♔c7 4 ♔d5 ♔b7 5 ♔c5 ♔a6 6 ♔c6** and the b-pawn falls.

33) White wins by **1 c5!** (1 cxb5? wins a pawn, but only draws after 1...♔e6 2 ♔g3 ♔d6 3 ♔h4 ♔c7, when Black will take both pawns) **1...♔f5 2 ♔g3 ♔f6 3 ♔h4 ♔f5** (White wins after 3...♔g6 4 c6, so Black cannot defend his h-pawn) **4 ♔xh5 ♔f6** and now White wins easily; for example, **5 ♔g4 ♔e5 6 ♔g5 ♔e6 7 ♔f4 ♔d5 8 ♔f5 ♔c6 9 ♔e6 ♔c7 10 ♔d5 ♔d7 11 c6+ ♔c7 12 ♔c5** and the b-pawn is lost.

34) If Black were to play, he would be in zugzwang and lose his pawn immediately. White can win by transferring the move to Black using a process called *triangulation*. After **1 ♔b2** (1 ♔a2 followed by 2 ♔b2 is just as good) **1...♔a6 2 ♔a2! ♔b5** (after 2...♔a7 3 ♔a3 White also wins the pawn) **3 ♔a3** it is now Black to play, and he loses his pawn and the game. The white king has moved in the triangle a3-b2-a2-a3 while Black has moved back and forth. The net result is to change the player to move.

35) White should not play 1 ♔e4? as he loses a pawn after 1...♔d6. Squares which a king dare not move to are called *mined*. Here e4 and c4 are mined for White, as Black's reply ...♔d6 works in either case. To win, White must play his king to the queenside while avoiding the mined squares, except if Black plays his king to d6: **1 ♔d3! ♔c7** (1...♔d6 loses to 2 ♔e4; it's OK to play ♔e4 when the black king is on d6, since then it is Black who is in zugzwang) **2 ♔c3! ♔d7 3 ♔b4! ♔d6** (or else ♔c5 at once) **4 ♔c4** (now it's Black to move) **4...♔d7 5 ♔c5 ♔c7 6 d6+ ♔d7 7 ♔d5** and White wins.

36) White can win. If you have an extra passed pawn far away from the other pawns then you almost always win. A distant passed pawn is called an *outside passed pawn* and it can be used to deflect the opponent's king so that your own king can get a clear run at the enemy pawns. Here's how it works: **1 ♔e3 ♔f5** (1...♔d5 2 ♔d3 is similar) **2 ♔f3 ♔f6 3 ♔e4 ♔e6 4 ♔d4 ♔d6 5 f5** (Black's king must deal with the passed f-pawn, allowing White to take the b5-pawn) **5...♔e7 6 ♔c5 ♔f6 7 ♔xb5 ♔xf5 8 ♔c6** and White promotes the b-pawn.

37) Even with equal material, an outside passed pawn is often a decisive advantage. White can indeed win in this position, but a little care is needed: **1 ♔d4!** (1 a5? is too slow and allows Black to exchange the h-pawn by 1...g4 2 ♔d4 h5 3 ♔e4 h4 4 ♔f4 g3) **1...h5** (1...♔c6 2 ♔e5 ♔b6 3 ♔f5 ♔a5 4 ♔g6 also wins easily) **2 ♔e4 g4 3 ♔f4**, followed by ♔g5, after which White takes both black pawns and then wins with his h-pawn.

38) The key idea is to prevent Black from creating his own passed pawn by ...g5. **1 h5!** (1 ♔e6? g5 and 1 c6? g5 both allow Black to draw) **1...♔d7 2 c6+ ♔c7 3 ♔c5!** (White cannot use his outside passed pawn to win as in the previous exercise, since 3 ♔e6? ♔xc6 4 ♔f7 ♔d7 5 ♔xg7 ♔e8 6 ♔xh6 ♔f8 only leads to a draw as in Exercise 12; instead, a different approach is necessary) **3...♔c8 4 ♔d6 ♔d8 5 c7+ ♔c8 6 ♔c6!** (it's zugzwang and now Black must commit suicide by pushing his g-pawn) **6...g5 7 hxg6 h5 8 g7 h4 9 g8♕#**.

39) At the moment White's g-pawn holds back all three enemy pawns. The winning idea is to stalemate Black's king and use zugzwang to force Black to push a pawn: **1 a5!** (1 ♔c6? ♔a7 2 ♔d6 doesn't work because White will not promote with check if Black's king is not on the back rank; then 2...h5! 3 gxh5 g4 4 h6 g3 5 h7 g2 6 h8♕ g1♕ leads to a drawn ending with equal material) **1...♔c8 2 a6 ♔b8 3 a7+ ♔a8 4 ♔a6** (forcing Black to self-destruct on the kingside) **4...h5 5 gxh5 f5 6 h6 f4 7 h7 f3 8 h8♕#**.

40) An extra outside passed pawn may not win if the last pawn is going to be a rook's pawn. Here Black can save the game: **1...♔e7! 2 ♔e4 ♔f6 3 ♔f4 ♔f7 4 ♔e5 ♔e7 5 ♔d5 ♔f6 6 ♔c5 ♔xf5 7 ♔b5 ♔e6 8 ♔xa5 ♔d7 9 ♔b6 ♔c8** and Black makes it back to the drawing square c8 just in time.

41) The active position of White's king allows him to break up the enemy pawns and win material: **1 f5! gxf5** (or else White takes on g6 and wins two pawns) **2 ♔xf5 ♔g7 3 ♔g5** (the h-pawn is doomed and this is enough to win) **3...f6+ 4 ♔xh5 ♔h7 5 ♔g4!** (not 5 g4? ♔g7 6 g5 fxg5 with a draw) **5...♔g6 6 ♔f4 ♔g7 7 ♔f5 ♔f7 8 h5 ♔g7 9 g4 ♔f7 10 h6** and the f-pawn falls as well, with an easy win for White.

42) 1 ♔d5? a5! wins for Black as 2 ♔c6? loses to 2...c4, so Black has time to bring his king across and win. 1 ♔b5? a5! is the same. Instead, White must use his own pawns as weapons to break up the enemy pawns, and he must do it straight away: **1 a5! ♔e5 2 axb6**

axb6 3 a4 (White's work is not yet finished; the second a-pawn must also be put to use) 3...♔d6 4 ♔b5 ♔c7 (4...♔d5 5 ♔xb6 c4 6 a5 c3 7 a6 c2 8 a7 c1♕ 9 a8♕+ is also a draw) 5 a5! bxa5 6 ♔xc5 and White wins Black's last pawn. When the enemy king is far away, your own pawns can often be used as battering-rams to smash down the enemy pawn-structure.

43) 1 ♔f5? ♔c3! 2 ♔e5 ♔b4 is a simple win for Black, while 1 ♔f3? loses to 1...♔d3! (heading for b5 while shouldering away the white king) 2 ♔f2 ♔c4 3 a6 (converting the b-pawn into a less useful a-pawn is often a good idea, but it doesn't work here) 3...bxa6 4 ♔e2 ♔c3 5 ♔d1 ♔b2 and the a-pawn can advance. Surprisingly, **1 ♔f4!** is the only move to draw. The king needs to be able to head for either c7 or c1, depending on Black's reply, and only the 'Goldilocks' move to the middle of the three squares keeps both options open. After **1...♔c3** (1...♔d3 allows 2 ♔e5! ♔c4 3 ♔d6 ♔b5 4 ♔c7 with a draw) **2 ♔e3! ♔b4 3 a6! bxa6 4 ♔d2 ♔b3 5 ♔c1** White reaches the drawing square c1.

44) White wins by **1 ♔f4!**, which confines Black's king and causes him to waste time getting his king out of the way of the h-pawn. After **1...♔h3 2 e4 ♔g2 3 e5 h4 4 e6 h3 5 e7 h2 6 e8♕ h1♕** (both sides have promoted, but this is an exceptional position in which White can win) **7 ♕e2+! ♔g1** (or 7...♔h3 8 ♕g4+ ♔h2 9 ♕g3#) **8 ♔g3!** it will be mate in a few moves. The idea of letting Black promote and then mating is a key idea in some pawn endings.

45) As in Exercise 43, the draw is based on using the white king to head towards two objectives at the same time. The first is to assist the c-pawn, and the second is to catch Black's pawn: **1 ♔f7! ♔b5** (1...h4 2 ♔e6 h3 3 c6 h2 4 c7 is also a draw, so Black takes time to restrain the c-pawn) **2 ♔e6!** (it's all a question of geometry: with the king on e6, White threatens both ♔f5 catching the h-pawn and ♔d6 supporting his own pawn) **2...h4** (2...♔xc5 3 ♔f5) **3 ♔d6** (not 3 ♔d5? h3, when Black will promote with check) **3...h3 4 c6 h2 5 c7 h1♕ 6 c8♕** with a draw.

46) 1 ♔d5 ♔c8 2 ♔c4! (2 ♔d6 ♔d8 3 c7+? ♔c8 leads nowhere as 4 ♔c6 stalemates Black, but as in Exercise 34 White can transfer the move to Black using triangulation; 2 ♔d4! ♔d8 3 ♔c4 is just as good) **2...♔d8** (2...♔c7 loses to 3 ♔c5 followed by ♔b6) **3 ♔d4 ♔c8 4 ♔d5** (the same position as after 1...♔c8 but now it is Black to play) **4...♔c7** (or 4...♔d8 5 ♔d6 ♔c8 6 c7 and White wins) **5 ♔c5** and Black is in zugzwang. He must move his king, and then 6 ♔b6 wins the a-pawn.

47) Exercise 40 was a draw, but here White wins. It may seem odd, but in positions like this it is generally better to have the outside passed pawn as far back as possible. We shall see why in a few moves: **1...♔e6 2 ♔e3 ♔f5 3 ♔f3!** (3 ♔d4? ♔xf4 4 ♔c5 ♔e5 5 ♔b5 ♔d6 6 ♔xa5 ♔c7 is a draw) **3...♔f6 4 ♔e4 ♔e6 5 ♔d4** (now is the time to make a run for the a-pawn, since White ends up a move ahead of the line after 3 ♔d4?) **5...♔f5 6 ♔c5 ♔xf4 7 ♔b5 ♔e5 8 ♔xa5 ♔d6** (Black could play ...♔d7 in the corresponding line with the pawn on f5, but here White can shoulder away the enemy king) **9 ♔b6! ♔d7 10 ♔b7** followed by pushing the a-pawn.

48) 1...b6?? is a blunder due to 2 b5!, when White promotes a pawn on a8 after 2...bxa5 3 bxa6 or 2...axb5 3 a6. You should always keep an eye open for breakthroughs, both for yourself and for your opponent. **1...♔g6!** is the correct move, and after **2 ♔f4 ♔f6** (Black slowly but surely utilizes his extra pawn) **3 ♔e4 ♔e6 4 ♔d4 ♔d6 5 ♔c4 ♔c6 6 ♔c3** (6 b5+ axb5+ 7 ♔b4 ♔d5 8 ♔xb5 ♔d4 9 ♔b4 c6 also wins for Black) **6...♔b5 7 ♔b3 c5 8 bxc5 ♔xc5** Black wins White's a-pawn in a couple of moves.

29

3 Minor-Piece Endings

Endings with bishops, knights and pawns are called *minor-piece endings*. This chapter is effectively four chapters rolled into one. First we consider pure knight endings, then pure bishop endings. The bishop endings are divided into two quite different sections, according to whether the bishops move on squares of the same colour or opposite colour. Finally, we investigate endings in which one side has a bishop and the other a knight.

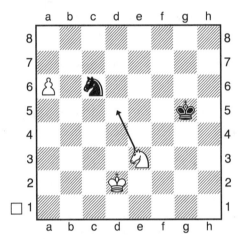

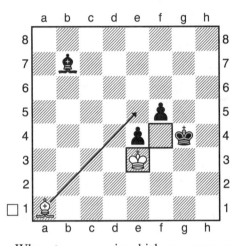

Knights are short-range pieces and have difficulties coping with passed pawns near the edge of the board, especially rook's pawns. Here White can exploit his pawn with the aid of some knight forks. 1 ♔c3? ♗f4! 2 ♘d5+ ♔e5 3 ♔c4 ♔d6 only draws, but **1 ♘d5!** wins, preventing 1...♔f5 due to 2 ♘e7+! ♗xe7 3 a7 and the pawn promotes. Therefore Black loses valuable time because he cannot immediately approach with his king. His best try is **1...♘a7**, to allow ...♔f5, but White wins in any case after **2 ♔d3 ♔f5 3 ♔c4 ♔e6 4 ♔c5 ♔d7 5 ♔b6 ♘c6 6 ♘e3** (heading for a5 to drive Black's knight away) **6...♔d6 7 ♘c4+ ♔d7 8 ♘a5 ♘e7** (after 8...♘xa5 9 a7 the pawn promotes) **9 ♔b7** (9 a7? ♘c8+ and ...♘xa7) **9...♘c8 10 ♘c4 ♔d8 11 ♘b6 ♘d6+ 12 ♔c6** followed by a7.

When two opposing bishops move on squares of different colours they are called *opposite-coloured bishops*. In the diagram White's bishop moves on dark squares (a *dark-squared bishop*) while Black's moves on light squares (a *light-squared bishop*). When there are no other pieces on the board, opposite-coloured bishops tend to lead to a draw, mainly because it's easy for passed pawns to get stuck. If Black were able to set his pawns in motion with ...f4+ then he would win, but White can prevent this by **1 ♗e5!**. Then White leaves his king on e3 and just moves his bishop up and down the h2-b8 diagonal. The opposite-coloured bishops mean that there is no way for Black to challenge White's blockade on the dark squares e3 and f4. The position is now a clear draw as Black can never advance his pawns.

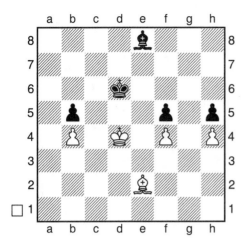

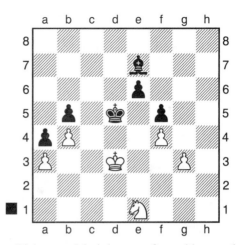

When the bishops move on squares of the same colour, we call them *same-coloured bishops*. Then much depends on how active each bishop is. Here Black's bishop moves on light squares, but the black pawns are stuck on squares of the same colour, limiting the bishop. A bishop obstructed by friendly pawns is called a *bad bishop*. In the diagram, Black can never move his king, as then the white king would advance by ♔c5 or ♔e5, winning a pawn at b5 or f5. It follows that he can only move his bishop. If it were Black to move, he would be in zugzwang and lose a pawn at once. By a clever manoeuvre, White can return to the diagram with Black to move: **1 ♗f3! ♗g6** (1...♗f7 loses to 2 ♗d1 since 2...♗e8 3 ♗e2 is zugzwang, while after 2...♗g6 3 ♗c2 ♗h7 4 ♗d3 White picks up the b5-pawn) **2 ♗d5 ♗e8** (2...♗h7 3 ♗f7 wins the h5-pawn) **3 ♗b3 ♗c6** (3...♗d7 is the same, while 3...♗g6 4 ♗c2 ♗h7 5 ♗d3 again costs Black the b5-pawn) **4 ♗d1 ♗e8 5 ♗e2** and now it's the diagram position but with Black to move. He will lose a pawn and the game. There's a resemblance between White's play here and the process of triangulation discussed in the chapter on king and pawn endings (see Exercise 34 on page 21).

Bishop and knight are of roughly equal value, but endgames favouring the bishop are more common than ones favouring the knight. Here Black has a winning position because all the white pawns are on dark squares and so can be attacked by the bishop. Moreover, the long-range bishop can create threats on both sides of the board, which White's short-range pieces will have trouble dealing with.

Black wins by **1...♗d8!** (intending ...♗b6 followed by ...♗f2; 1...♗f6? 2 ♘c2 followed by 3 ♘e3+ lets White escape) **2 ♘f3** (preparing ♘d2-f1 to defend the g3-pawn; 2 ♘c2 ♗b6 3 ♘e3+ can now be met by 3...♗xe3 4 ♔xe3 ♔c4, winning for Black) **2...♗f6** (now the threat is ...♗b2; notice how the bishop creates threats first on one side of the board and then on the other, stretching White's forces to the limit) **3 ♔c2 ♗g7** (now White is in zugzwang; 3...♔e4 is inaccurate as 4 ♘g5+ forces the king back to d5) **4 ♔b1** (4 ♘d2 ♔d4 followed by ...♔e3 is also winning for Black) **4...♔d4 5 ♘d2 ♗f2 6 ♘f1 ♔e4**, followed by ...♔f3, and Black has an easy win once his king advances to attack the pawns.

Exercises

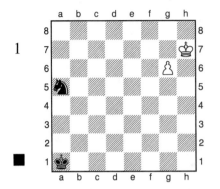

1

Can Black stop the pawn and draw?

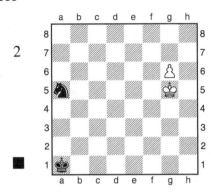

2

It's the same as Exercise 1, except the white king is on g5. Can Black draw now?

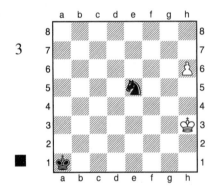

3

How does Black save the game?

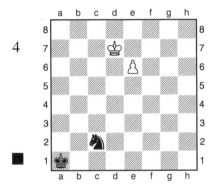

4

How can Black draw?

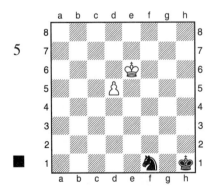

5

Only one move draws. Is it 1...♞d2, 1...♞e3 or 1...♞g3?

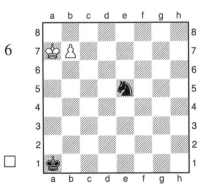

6

Which is the correct move: 1 b8♛, 1 ♔b8 or 1 ♔b6?

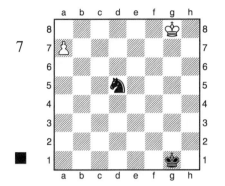

7

Which move should Black play: 1...♘c7 or 1...♘b6?

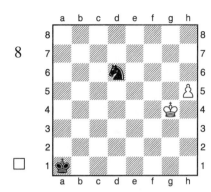

8

Which move wins: 1 h6, 1 ♔g5 or 1 ♔f4? Now suppose the black king starts on b3; is it still a win?

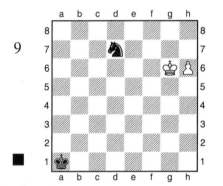

9

Black is to play. Is this a draw or a win for White?

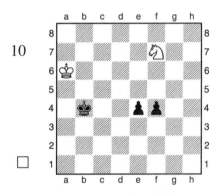

10

Find the drawing move for White.

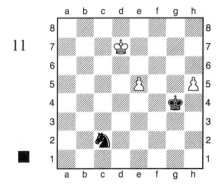

11

How does Black draw?

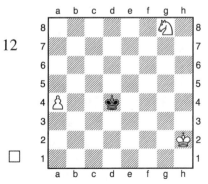

12

Is the correct move 1 ♘f6, 1 ♘e7 or 1 a5?

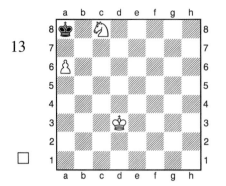

13

Which move wins: 1 a7, 1 ♘d4 or 1 ♔c4?

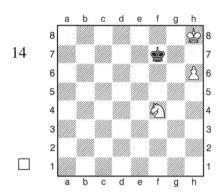

14

Which is the best move: 1 ♔h7, 1 h7 or 1 ♘e6?

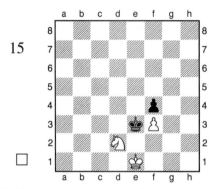

15

White has an extra piece, but can he win?

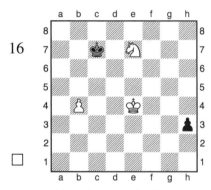

16

How should White stop the h-pawn: 1 ♔f3 or 1 ♘f5?

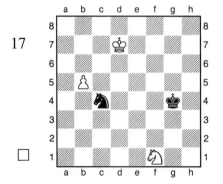

17

Find the winning move for White.

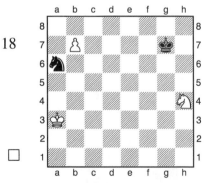

18

Should White play 1 ♘f5+, 1 ♔a4 or 1 ♔b2?

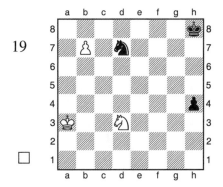

19

Bearing in mind Exercise 18, find the winning move for White.

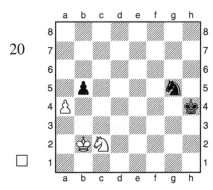

20

On general principles, should White play 1 a5 or 1 axb5?

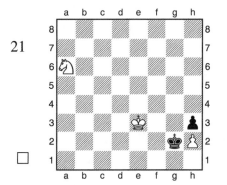

21

Black is about to capture White's pawn. Does this mean that it is a draw?

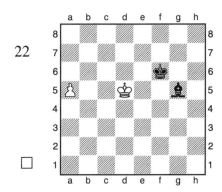

22

Can White win?

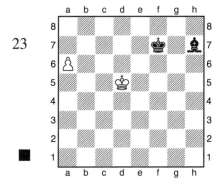

23

Can Black save the game?

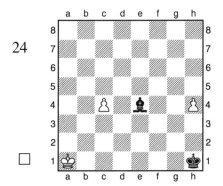

24

Which pawn should White push?

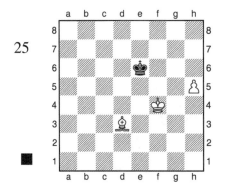

25

Can Black draw this apparently hopeless position?

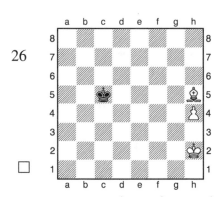

26

Should White play 1 ♗g6, 1 ♗e8 or 1 ♗f3?

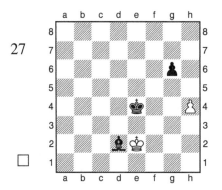

27

How does White draw here?

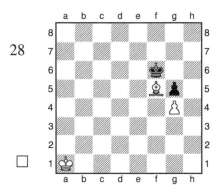

28

White needs to win the g5-pawn to win the game. Is this possible?

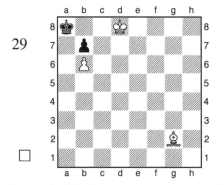

29

Does 1 ♗c6 lead a win, a loss or a draw?

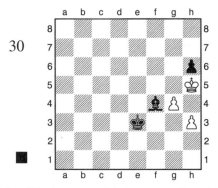

30

Can Black prevent his last pawn from being exchanged by h4 and g5?

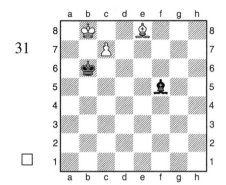

31

Find the winning plan for White.

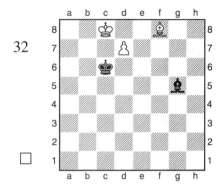

32

This is the previous exercise shifted one square to the right. Is it still a win?

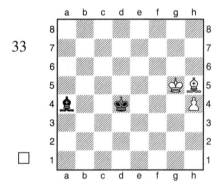

33

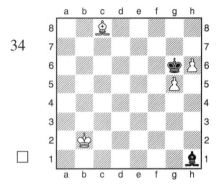

34

Should White play 1 ♗g4 or 1 ♗g6, and why?

Find the winning move for White.

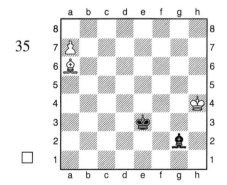

35

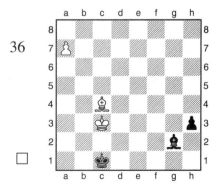

36

What should Black play after 1 ♔g3?

How does White win?

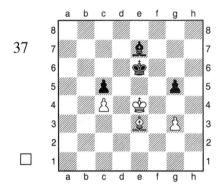

37

How does White win a pawn and the game?

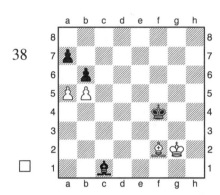

38

Should White play 1 axb6, 1 a6 or 1 ♗xb6?

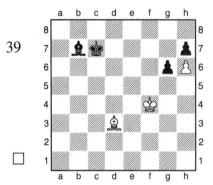

39

Is the winning move 1 ♗xg6 or 1 ♔e5?

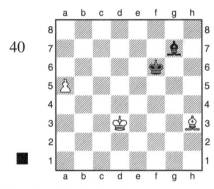

40

How does Black draw?

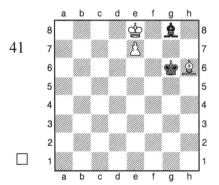

41

How does White win?

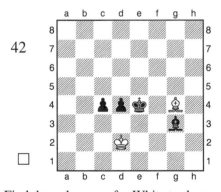

42

Find the only move for White to draw.

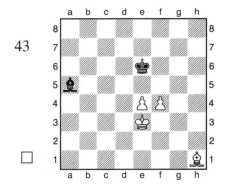

43

Which move wins: 1 e5, 1 f5+ or 1 ♔d4?

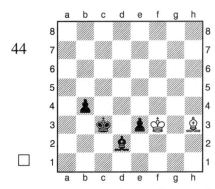

44

Should White play 1 ♔e2, 1 ♗f5 or 1 ♗e6?

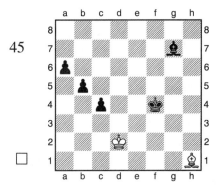

45

Find the correct drawing plan for White.

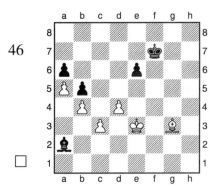

46

Which is the only move to win for White?

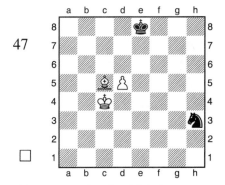

47

Which move wins for White?

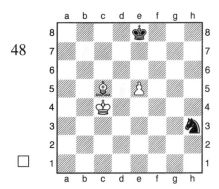

48

Can White win in this slightly different position?

49

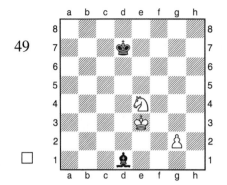

How does White win?

50

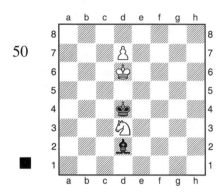

Should Black play 1...♗a5 or 1...♗g5?

51

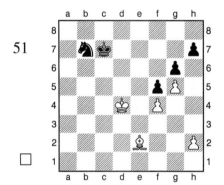

Which plan is correct: 1 ♗c4 to play ♗g8 and ♗xh7, or 1 ♔e5 heading towards g7?

52

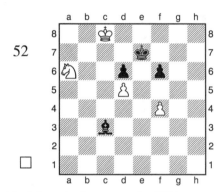

Find the winning move for White.

53

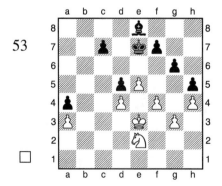

Which is White's best move?

54

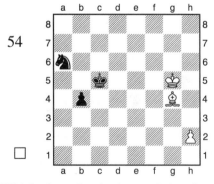

Which player is winning, or is it a draw?

55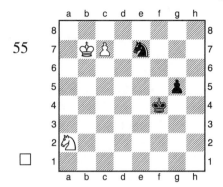

Which is the correct move: 1 c8♕, 1 ♘c3 or 1 ♘b4?

56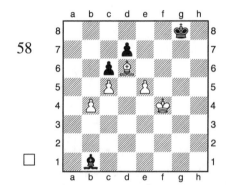

Can Black save the game by 1...♘d5?

57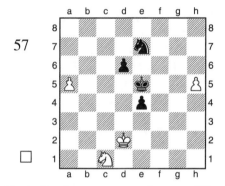

Both sides have two passed pawns. Who has the advantage and why?

58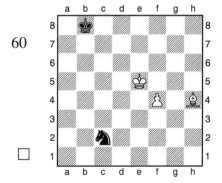

Which move is best: 1 b5, 1 e6 or 1 ♔g5?

59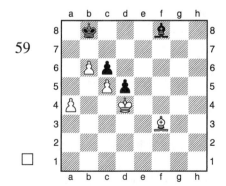

Find the winning move for White.

60

Should White play 1 f5, 1 ♔e4 or 1 ♗f2?

Solutions to Minor-Piece Endings Exercises

1) Black can stop the pawn by racing back with his knight: **1...♘c6 2 g7 ♘e7** and White has nothing better than **3 g8♕ ♘xg8 4 ♔xg8** with a draw.

2) Now Black cannot draw. After **1...♘c6 2 ♔f6!** the king prevents the knight from approaching so Black cannot stop the pawn queening. The king is a powerful piece in the endgame and is especially effective when combating an enemy knight.

3) Black draws by **1...♘f7!** (just stopping the pawn by 1...♘g6? isn't good enough and White wins by 2 h7 ♔b2 3 ♔g4 ♔c3 4 ♔g5 ♘h8 5 ♔f6 ♔d4 6 ♔g7 ♔e5 7 ♔xh8 ♔f6 8 ♔g8) **2 h7 ♘g5+** and the pawn falls. It's not surprising that knight forks are important in knight endings!

4) **1...♘e3!** (attacking the pawn by 1...♘d4? looks natural, but after 2 e7 there is no way to prevent promotion; 1...♘b4? is also wrong because of 2 ♔d6! and once again the pawn runs through) **2 e7 ♘d5!** (not 2...♘g4?, when 3 ♔e6! stops the knight from moving to f6 and wins, providing another example of the effective use of the king) **3 e8♕ ♘f6+** and Black saves the game with a fork.

5) It can be quite hard to work out how to stop a pawn with a knight. Here 1...♘e3? is wrong due to 2 d6 ♘c4 3 d7, and 1...♘g3? loses to the surprising 2 ♔e5! (but not 2 d6? ♘e4, which is a draw as in the main line) and the king shuts all routes by which the knight might stop the pawn. The correct line is **1...♘d2! 2 d6** (or else ...♘c4 draws) **2...♘e4** (2...♘b3 also draws, but attacking the pawn is more forcing) **3 d7 ♘c5+** followed by ...♘xd7.

6) Sometimes you need to be creative to find the right move. 1 b8♕? ♘c6+ is an immediate draw, while 1 ♔b6? ♘d7+ 2 ♔c7 ♘c5! 3 b8♕ ♘a6+ also doesn't win. The winning move **1 ♔b8!** looks odd, because White blocks his own pawn, but now the knight cannot stop the pawn. The immediate threat is 2 ♔c7, and after **1...♘d7+** (1...♘c6+ 2 ♔c7 ♘b4 and now 3 ♔b6! wins, but not 3 b8♕? ♘a6+) **2 ♔c8!** (2 ♔c7? ♘c5 is again a draw) **2...♘b6+ 3 ♔d8** the pawn reaches the eighth rank.

7) Rook's pawns offer more winning chances, since if the pawn is on the seventh rank the knight can easily get trapped in the corner in front of the pawn. Black must take care here, and the key defensive idea is that of a *barrier*. After **1...♘b6!**, the white king cannot move to d6 or e7 because of the fork ...♘c8+, while d5 and d7 are directly covered. There is an invisible barrier to the white king extending from d5 to d7, and the only way the white king can attack the enemy knight is to sneak along the eighth rank via d8. This route along the edge of the board does nothing to block the approach of Black's king, and he draws by **2 ♔f8 ♔f2 3 ♔e8 ♔e3 4 ♔d8 ♔d4 5 ♔c7 ♔c5**, when he is just in time to avoid having to play ...♘a8, which would lead to the knight being trapped. 1...♘c7? loses because there is no barrier, and White can attack the knight more quickly by 2 ♔f7 ♔f2 3 ♔e7 ♔e3 4 ♔d7. Then 4...♘a8 5 ♔c6 ♔d4 6 ♔b7 ♔c5 7 ♔xa8 ♔b6 8 ♔b8 wins for White.

8) 1 ♔g5? ♘f7+ 2 ♔g6 ♘e5+ 3 ♔g7 ♘g4 is a draw, as the pawn can never make it to h6 without being taken, and 1 ♔f4? ♘f7 is similar. However, **1 h6!** wins, because after **1...♘f7** (after 1...♘e4 White wins by 2 ♔f5! ♘d6+ 3 ♔g6, but not 2 h7? ♘f6+ and the pawn is lost) **2 h7 ♔b2 3 ♔f5 ♔c3 4 ♔f6 ♘h8 5 ♔g7** the knight is trapped in the corner and lost. If the black king starts on b3, then it is only a draw since Black's king is close enough to trap

42

White's king on h8: **1 h6 ♘f7 2 h7 ♚c4 3 ♚f5 ♚d5 4 ♚f6 ♘h8 5 ♚g7 ♚e6 6 ♚xh8 ♚f7** stalemate.

9) Perhaps surprisingly, this is a draw. At first sight, White can drive the knight away and win after **1...♘f8+ 2 ♚f7** (2 ♚g7 ♘e6+ followed by ...♘f8 or ...♘g5 also holds up the pawn) **2...♘h7 3 ♚g7 ♘g5 4 ♚g6** and Black cannot cover h7 directly. However, the cunning trick **4...♘e6! 5 h7 ♘f8+** saves the day. The basic rule is that **a knight can stop a rook's pawn on the sixth rank** provided it can control the square immediately in front of the pawn. In Exercise 8 (after 1 h6!), the pawn was also on the sixth rank but Black could not control the square in front of the pawn (h7) and so lost.

10) White must win one of the pawns or he is doomed. By chasing them up the board he eventually picks one up with a fork: **1 ♘g5!** (1 ♘d6? e3 is hopeless for White) **1...e3 2 ♘e6! f3** (2...e2 3 ♘xf4 e1♛ 4 ♘d3+ is also drawn) **3 ♘d4! f2 4 ♘c2+** and **5 ♘xe3**, capturing one pawn and halting the other.

11) 1...♚xh5? fails because after 2 e6 ♘e3 3 e7 ♘d5 White promotes with check, while 1...♘e3? loses to 2 h6 ♘c4 3 e6 as the two pawns are too strong. **1...♚g5!** is the key move, holding up the h-pawn without allowing the e-pawn to promote with check. Then **2 e6** (2 h6 ♚xh6 is a draw as White still does not promote with check) **2...♘e3! 3 e7 ♘d5 4 e8♛** (not check!) **4...♘f6+ 5 ♚e7 ♘xe8 6 ♚xe8 ♚xh5** leads to a draw.

12) In order to win, White must securely defend the pawn with his knight, when he can bring his king across to support the pawn. The key word here is 'securely', since a defence with the knight in front of the pawn (on c5 or b6) is not secure, while a defence from behind (on c3 or b2) is secure. We shall see why in a moment. **1 ♘f6!** (1 a5? ♚c5 2 ♘e7 ♚b5 3 ♘c6 ♚xc6 is a draw, and 1 ♘e7? ♚c4 2 ♘c8 ♚b4 3 ♘b6 ♚a5 is also a draw because Black genuinely threatens to take the knight) **1...♚c4 2 ♘e4** (the knight is just in time to set up a secure defence from c3) **2...♚b4 3 ♘c3!** and Black cannot take the knight since then the a-pawn rushes forward, so he can do nothing but wait while the white king approaches. That's why White needs to defend the pawn from behind; if the knight is in front of the pawn, Black can take the knight and still stop the pawn.

13) Knight and pawn normally win against a lone king provided the pawn is not lost straight away, but there are exceptions. 1 a7? is a mistake, since 1...♚b7 2 ♚c4 ♚a8 3 ♚c5 ♚b7 4 ♚b5 ♚a8 is a draw; if the white king moves any closer it is stalemate, while otherwise White can never move the knight. 1 ♚d4? also doesn't work, as 1...♚b8 2 ♘d6 (2 a7+ ♚b7 is a draw as after 1 a7?) 2...♚a7 wins the pawn. **1 ♚c4!** is the right move, and after **1...♚b8 2 ♘d6** (2 ♘b6 and 2 ♘e7 are just as good) **2...♚a7 3 ♚b5** the king is in time to defend the pawn. Then White wins easily; for example, **3...♚a8 4 ♚b6 ♚b8 5 ♘b5 ♚a8 6 ♘c7+ ♚b8 7 a7+** and the pawn promotes.

14) This exercise involves another of the rare exceptions in which knight and pawn don't beat a lone king. 1 h7? ♚f8 is a draw because White cannot drive Black's king away from the squares f7 and f8, which allow him to keep the white king boxed in on h8. It looks as if White can use his knight to force the enemy king away, but it never works; for example, 2 ♘e6+ ♚f7 and now if White could just pass, Black would have to allow ♚g8, but White has to move the knight away, after which Black replies ...♚f8. However White plays, the knight is

43

always on the wrong foot to control f7 or f8. 1 ♘e6? is also bad due to 1...♚g6! (1...♚xe6? loses to 2 ♚g7) 2 h7 ♚f7 with the same situation as after 1 h7?. The win is **1 ♚h7! ♚f8** (or else 2 ♚g8 followed by h7) **2 ♚g6** and now that the white king has escaped from the corner there are several ways to win; for example, **2...♚g8 3 ♘d3 ♚h8 4 ♘e5 ♚g8 5 h7+ ♚h8 6 ♘f7#**.

15) White can win, but because the knight is tied down to the defence of his last pawn, he must manoeuvre solely with his king. **1 ♚d1 ♚f2** (after 1...♚d3 2 ♘f1 ♚c3 3 ♚e2 White frees his knight, simplifying the win) **2 ♚c2 ♚e2 3 ♚c3 ♚e3 4 ♚c4!** (the key idea is that White can abandon the knight if his king is well-placed) **4...♚xd2** (otherwise ♚d4 followed by ♚e4 wins in any case) **5 ♚d4 ♚e2 6 ♚e4** followed by ♚xf4, when White promotes his pawn and wins.

16) 1 ♚f3? ♚b6 draws because White cannot defend the pawn with his knight from behind; for example, 2 ♚g3 ♚b5 3 ♘d5 ♚c4 and the pawn falls. **1 ♘f5!** is correct. White should use his knight to hold up the h-pawn and his king to support the b-pawn rather than the other way around. Then **1...h2 2 ♘g3 ♚c6 3 ♚d4 ♚b5 4 ♚c3** (this would be a draw without the pieces on the kingside, but here White wins) **4...♚b6 5 ♚c4 ♚c6 6 b5+ ♚b6 7 ♚b4 ♚b7 8 ♚c5 ♚c7 9 b6+ ♚b7 10 ♚b5 ♚b8 11 ♚c6 ♚c8 12 b7+ ♚b8 13 ♘h1!** (the knight provides a waiting move to force Black to move his king away from b8) **13...♚a7 14 ♚c7** wins for White.

17) **1 ♘e3+!** (White uses a fork to draw the enemy knight away and free the pawn to advance) **1...♘xe3 2 b6 ♘c4** (there's no way for the black knight to stop the pawn) **3 b7 ♘e5+ 4 ♚c7** and the pawn promotes.

18) Black's knight is creating a barrier (see Exercise 7) to the white king, since 1 ♚a4? and 1 ♚b3? both lose the pawn to 1...♘c5+. 1 ♘f5+? ♚f7 is also wrong as it just chases the black king towards White's pawn. Amazingly, the only move to win is **1 ♚b2!**, going around the barrier on a4, b4 and b3. Then **1...♚f6 2 ♚c3 ♚e6** (2...♚g5 3 ♘g2 doesn't help Black) **3 ♚c4 ♚d6 4 ♚b5 ♘b8 5 ♚b6** (White's king has reached an active position, allowing it to support the pawn; now he only has to bring his knight in to finish the job) **5...♘d7+ 6 ♚a7 ♚c7 7 ♘g6 ♚d6 8 ♘f8** drives the enemy knight away and the pawn promotes.

19) White's b-pawn is far advanced, but first he must neutralize Black's h-pawn. 1 ♘f4? stops the pawn but then the knight must stay on the kingside to hold up the h-pawn, and White cannot win using only his king. The winning line is **1 ♘e5!** (White uses a deflection idea to boost his knight towards g6) **1...♘b8 2 ♘g6+** (now White wins the h-pawn) **2...♚g7 3 ♘xh4 ♘a6** (the best defence as it prevents both ♚a4 and ♚b4), reaching the position of Exercise 18, in which White can win by **4 ♚b2!**.

20) It's tempting to take the pawn, but White can easily pick up the b-pawn using his king or knight, so both moves will lead to the eventual capture of Black's pawn. The deciding factor is the general principle that knights have trouble coping with rook's pawns, and on this basis it's better to play a5. The analysis runs **1 a5!** (1 axb5? ♘e4 2 b6 ♘d6! 3 ♚c3 ♚g5 4 ♚d4 ♚f6 5 ♚d5 ♚e7 and now 6 ♚c6 runs into 6...♘c4 7 b7 ♘a5+, so Black gets his king to d7 and draws) **1...♘e6 2 a6 ♘c7 3 a7 ♚g5 4 ♘d4 ♚f6 5 ♘xb5 ♘a8 6 ♚c3** (White arrives with his king in time to win) **6...♚e6 7 ♚c4 ♚d7 8 ♚c5 ♚c8 9 ♚c6 ♚d8 10 ♚b7 ♚d7 11**

♘c3! (11 ♔xa8? ♔c8 is a draw as in Exercise 14 after 1 h7?) **11...♘c7 12 ♘d5 ♘a8 13 ♘b6+** and White wins.

21) It is not a draw, as White can play for mate. **1 ♘c5!** (the knight must rush back as quickly as possible) **1...♔xh2 2 ♔f2** (Black's king is boxed in the corner) **2...♔h1 3 ♘e4 ♔h2** (3...h2 is met by 4 ♘g3#) **4 ♘d2 ♔h1 5 ♘f1 h2 6 ♘g3#**. This mating idea doesn't arise very often as it only works against a rook's pawn on the sixth rank. However, some positions can only be won using it, so it's certainly worth knowing.

22) White can win. It's usually easy to see if a bishop can stop a lone pawn, but there are a few positions where you need to think. Here White can use his king to prevent the bishop from moving to the g1-a7 diagonal. **1 ♔e4! ♗h4** (now Black intends ...♗f2) **2 ♔f3!** and the bishop cannot stop the pawn from promoting.

23) Black cannot prevent promotion, but he can draw all the same. After **1...♗d3!** (1...♗f5! 2 a7 ♗h3 is also good) **2 a7 ♗f1!** (2...♗e2? 3 ♔e4! ♗f1 4 ♔f3! prevents the skewer and wins) **3 a8♕ ♗g2+** Black wins the new-born queen with a skewer and draws.

24) A lone bishop has more trouble stopping two pawns, but White must choose the right pawn to advance. 1 c5? ♗f3! is only a draw, because neither h5 nor c6 is the last chance for the bishop to stop that particular pawn. Then 2 h5 ♗xh5 3 c6 ♗g4 and 2 c6 ♗xc6 3 h5 ♗e4 are safe for Black, while bringing the king up is too slow. **1 h5!** wins, because once the pawn is on h6, the bishop can never leave the b1-h7 diagonal, so the c-pawn can run through unhindered. Then **1...♔g2 2 h6 ♗f3 3 c5 ♗f4 4 c6 ♔e5** (Black is one move too slow to stop the c-pawn with his king) **5 c7 ♗f5 6 h7** promotes one of the pawns. The main point here is that if the square in front of the pawn is the last chance for the bishop to stop it, then the bishop will be tied to one diagonal.

BAD BISHOP

45

25) Normally White's material advantage would win easily, but this is an exception. If White has an h-pawn plus a light-squared bishop, then the defender can draw provided he can get his king to h8. **1...♔f7!** (1...♔f6? is wrong since 2 h6 ♔f7 3 ♗h7! prevents Black's king from getting to h8, and then 3...♔f6 4 ♔g4 ♔e6 5 ♔g5 ♔f7 6 ♔f5 ♔f8 7 ♔f6 ♔e8 8 ♗g6+ followed by h7 wins) **2 h6 ♔g8! 3 ♔g5 ♔h8 4 ♔g6 ♔g8 5 ♗c4+ ♔h8** and it's a draw because the danger of stalemate means that White can never force the enemy king out from the corner. This idea, called the *rook's pawn and wrong bishop draw*, has saved countless games. The basic rule is that **♔+♗+♙ vs ♔ with a rook's pawn and a bishop which does not control the pawn's promotion square is a draw if the defender can get his king to the promotion square**.

26) From the previous exercise, we know that it will be a draw if Black's king can reach h8, but it's not easy to see which move is necessary to prevent this. After 1 ♗e8? ♔d6! 2 h5 ♔e7 3 h6 ♔f8! (not 3...♔xe8? 4 h7) White cannot prevent the king from reaching h8, and 1 ♗f3? ♔d6 2 h5 ♔e7 3 h6 ♔f7! (3...♔f8? 4 ♗d5 and 3...♔f6? 4 ♗h5 both lose) also doesn't work. The correct method is **1 ♗g6! ♔d6 2 h5 ♔e7 3 h6 ♔f8** (3...♔f6 4 ♗h5 puts Black in zugzwang and next move h7 will promote the pawn) **4 ♗h7!** (blocking the king's path) **4...♔f7 5 ♔g3 ♔f6 6 ♔g4** and White is just in time to prevent ...♔g5. He now wins as in the previous exercise (after 1...♔f6?).

27) 1 ♔xd2? loses to the shouldering-away move **1...♔f3!** (not 1...♔f4? 2 h5 gxh5 3 ♔e2, reaching the drawing square f1), when 2 ♔e1 ♔g4 and 2 h5 gxh5 3 ♔e1 ♔g2 are both hopeless for White. White can only draw by **1 h5! gxh5** (1...g5 2 ♔xd2 is also a draw) **2 ♔f2!** (2 ♔f1! is just as good, but not 2 ♔xd2? ♔f3! 3 ♔e1 ♔g2, when Black wins) **2...h4 3 ♔g2** and the king reaches h1, with a rook's pawn plus wrong bishop draw.

28) If Black could simply pass, White would never be able to capture the g5-pawn, but by using zugzwang White can force Black's king away from the pawn and win it: **1 ♔b2 ♔e5 2 ♔c3 ♔f6 3 ♔d4 ♔f7 4 ♔e5 ♔g7 5 ♗b1 ♔h6 6 ♔f5** and the pawn falls, when White wins easily.

29) **1 ♗c6** should lead to a draw, but as the position is a draw in any case White might as well try it since it sets the trap 1...bxc6? 2 ♔c7 c5 3 b7+ ♔a7 4 b8♕+ ♔a6 5 ♕b6#. The correct defence is **1...♔b8!**, when Black is genuinely threatening to take the bishop. After **2 ♗f3 ♔a8**, for example, White cannot make progress as playing his king to c7 or c8 stalemates Black.

30) There appears to be no way to prevent h4 and g5, but Black can win with a surprise bishop sacrifice: **1...♗g5! 2 h4 ♗f4! 3 hxg5** (3 ♔g6 ♔xg4 is no better) **3...hxg5** and now White is in zugzwang and must surrender his g-pawn, after which Black wins easily using his own pawn.

31) The key idea is for White to drive the enemy bishop off the c8-h3 diagonal by playing his own bishop to c8. There are various routes to reach c8, all of them equally good. One possibility is **1 ♗h5 ♗h3 2 ♗f3 ♗f5 3 ♗b7 ♗h3 4 ♗c8 ♗f1 5 ♗g4** and Black's bishop must now cover c8 along the short a6-c8 diagonal rather than the longer h3-c8 diagonal. A diagonal with three or fewer squares is not safe and White can expel the bishop from this diagonal and promote his pawn: **5...♗a6 6 ♗e2 ♗b7 7 ♗f1** (Black is in zugzwang) **7...♔c6 8 ♗g2+**

and **9 ♗xb7**. The basic principle is that when you are holding up a pawn with a bishop, the longer the diagonal occupied by the bishop, the safer it is.

32) This position is a draw because the two diagonals leading to d8 are both long enough for Black's bishop to avoid being chased off: **1 ♗g7 ♗h4 2 ♗e5 ♗g5 3 ♗c7 ♗h4 4 ♗d8 ♗e1** (from here Black is ready to move to a5 or h4; playing 4...♗f2 or 4...♗g3 is just as good) **5 ♗g5 ♗a5 6 ♗d2 ♗c7 7 ♗e3** (in the previous exercise Black was in zugzwang in the analogous position, but here he has one safe square left for his bishop) **7...♗a5!** and White cannot win.

33) White should play **1 ♗g4!** (the analogous 1 ♗g6 ♗d1 2 ♗f5? doesn't work as 2...♔e5 3 ♗g4 ♗xg4 4 ♔xg4 ♔f6 draws) **1...♗e8 2 ♗f5!** (by playing his bishop to g6, White drives Black's bishop off the h5-e8 diagonal without blocking his own pawn) **2...♔e5 3 ♗g6 ♗a4 4 h5 ♗b3 5 h6 ♗g8** (this last-ditch defence doesn't hold White up for long) **6 ♗f5!** (now Black is in zugzwang and must allow the white king to occupy f6) **6...♔d6 7 ♔f6** followed by ♔g7 and the pawn will promote. Driving off an enemy bishop without blocking your own pawn (as with ♗g4-f5-g6 here) is one of the main themes in the ending of ♗+♙ vs ♗.

34) White wins with the bishop sacrifice **1 ♗f5+!** (not 1 ♔c3? ♗e4! 2 ♔d4 ♔xg5, when Black captures both white pawns) **1...♔f7** (after 1...♔xf5 2 h7 the h-pawn promotes) **2 g6+ ♔f8 3 g7+** and a pawn promotes.

35) After **1 ♔g3**, the only way to draw is **1...♗a8!** (1...♗c6? loses to 2 ♗f1! ♔d4 3 ♗g2) **2 ♗f1 ♔d4! 3 ♗g2 ♔c5 4 ♗xa8 ♔b6** and Black wins the pawn since the white bishop is blocking the promotion square. That's why the black bishop had to go to a8 on the first move.

36) Black is threatening to play ...h2 so White must act quickly. **1 ♗f1!** amusingly paralyses Black's bishop and pawn. The pawn cannot move as it must defend the bishop, while if the bishop moves White plays ♗xh3, followed by ♔d4 and ♗e6-d5, winning. So Black can only move his king, but then **1...♔d1** (or 1...♔b1 2 ♗xg2 hxg2 3 a8♕ g1♕ 4 ♕b7+ ♔c1 5 ♕b2+ ♔d1 6 ♕d2#) **2 ♗xg2 hxg2 3 a8♕ g1♕ 4 ♕a1+** costs Black his queen.

37) **1 g4!** is the decisive move, fixing both black pawns on dark squares where they can be attacked by White's bishop. Indeed, Black is in immediate zugzwang. If he moves the king, White plays ♔d5 or ♔f5 winning a pawn, while a bishop move leaves c5 or g5 undefended. White then wins provided he takes a little care; for example, **1...♗f8 2 ♗xg5 ♗g7 3 ♗e3 ♗f8 4 g5 ♗d6 5 ♗f2** (Black is in zugzwang, as allowing ♔d5 would lose the other pawn, so he must permit the white king to move to f4) **5...♗e7 6 ♔f4 ♗d6+ 7 ♔g4** followed by ♔h5 and g6, when the passed pawn is too strong.

38) 1 axb6? axb6 2 ♗xb6 ♔e5 gives Black plenty of time to get his king back to stop the b-pawn, with an easy draw. 1 a6? is also wrong as 1...♗e3 prevents the ♗xb6 sacrifice. Then 2 ♗g3+ ♔e4 3 ♗b8 ♗f4! 4 ♗xa7 ♗c7! traps the white bishop, after which Black plays his king back and takes the white pawns. The win is **1 ♗xb6! ♗d2** (after 1...axb6 2 a6 the a-pawn promotes) **2 a6** (2 ♗c7+ ♔e4 3 b6 also wins) **2...♔e5 3 ♗xa7 ♔d6 4 ♗b6** followed by a7 and the pawn promotes.

39) Black's pawns are vulnerable to attack from both bishop and king, so White wins even though he is a pawn down. However, he must find the right first move. **1 ♔e5!** (1 ♗xg6?

♔d7 2 ♗xh7 ♚e7 is only a draw) is correct. The king advances to g7 to shoulder away the enemy king, and then White takes the pawns with his bishop. **1...♚d7 2 ♔f6 ♚e8 3 ♔g7 ♗d5** (Black cannot bring his king any closer while the white king occupies g7) **4 ♗xg6+! ♚e7 5 ♗xh7** followed by a bishop move and then h7.

40) The ending of ♗+♙ vs ♗ is almost always a draw if there are opposite-coloured bishops. The defender need only use his bishop to cover a square the pawn has to cross, and then he can give up the bishop for the pawn when it reaches that square. Even in the unfavourable position of the diagram, Black's bishop can manoeuvre to cover a7. **1...♗f8!** (1...♗h6? is bad since after 2 a6 the white king prevents ...♗e3) **2 ♔c4** (trying to stop ...♗c5) **2...♗d6** (2...♗h6 also draws) **3 a6 ♗b8 4 ♚b5 ♗a7** and Black can keep his bishop on the g1-a7 diagonal.

41) This is one of the extremely rare winning positions with ♗+♙ vs ♗ and opposite-coloured bishops. Thanks to the unfavourable position of both black pieces, White wins by **1 ♔f8! ♗f7 2 ♗g5!** (not 2 ♗g7? ♚h7! 3 ♔xf7 with stalemate), when Black is in an odd zugzwang and cannot prevent the pawn from promoting in a move or two.

42) In order to draw, White must force the c-pawn onto a dark square so that he can blockade the pawns with his king and bishop. **1 ♗e6! c3+** (1...♗f4+ 2 ♔c2 d3+ 3 ♔c3 d2 4 ♔c2 is also a draw as White just keeps his bishop on the d1-h5 diagonal) **2 ♔c2** (2 ♔e2? d3+ wins for Black) **2...♗e5** (defending c3 and so threatening ...d3+) **3 ♗c4!** and White draws as Black cannot lift White's blockade of d3.

43) Connected passed pawns do sometimes win with opposite-coloured bishops, but only if they do not get blockaded. If you have the extra pawns, it's best to keep them on the same coloured squares as the enemy bishop (note this rule is the opposite of that for same-coloured bishops). Here 1 f5+? ♚e5 followed by ...♗d8 freezes the pawns in place, while 1 ♔d4? ♗b6+ 2 ♔c4 ♗c7 3 e5 (3 f5+ ♚e5 is also a blockade) 3...♗xe5 is also a draw. White wins by **1 e5!** (if Black had time to play ...♗c7 and ...♗xe5 then he would draw, but 1...♗c7 is met by 2 ♔e4) **1...♔f5 2 ♗b7 ♗b6+ 3 ♔f3 ♗c7 4 ♗c8+ ♔g6 5 f5+ ♔f7 6 ♗e6+ ♚e7 7 ♔e4** followed by ♔d5 and f6+, and the pawns are too strong.

44) Bishop and two disconnected passed pawns vs opposite-coloured bishop may be a draw or a win. It is better for the side with the pawns to have as many files between them as possible, but in this exercise they are just close enough for White to draw. **1 ♔e2!** (not 1 ♗f5? b3 2 ♔e2 ♔b2! and Black wins after 3 ♗e6 ♔c2 4 ♗f5+ ♚c1 or 3 ♗d1 ♔a1, when the b-pawn promotes, while 1 ♗e6? b3 2 ♔e2 ♔c2! is similar) **1...b3 2 ♔d1!** (preventing ...♔c2, which would win as in the previous note) **2...♔b2** (2...♔d3 3 ♗f5+ ♔d4 4 ♔e2 is also a draw) **3 ♗e6! ♔a2** (if 3...♔c3 then 4 ♗f5) **4 ♗f7** and Black cannot make progress as the b-pawn is pinned. The last winning try is **4...♔a3**, but then **5 ♗g6! b2 6 ♗b1** draws.

45) White would prefer Black's pawns to be on dark squares so that he can blockade them. Right now Black's king cannot defend them, so by attacking them with his bishop White can force them to advance: **1 ♗b7! a5 2 ♗a6** (2 ♗c6 b4 3 ♗b5 is equally good) **2...c3+ 3 ♔c2 b4 4 ♗b5!** (White must not allow ...a4 followed by ...b3+) **4...♔e3 5 ♗a4** (despite being three pawns down, White has a blockade, although he has to take a little care) **5...♔d4 6 ♗e8 ♔c4 7 ♗f7+!** (7 ♗a4? ♗f6 puts White in zugzwang, since 8 ♗b3+ ♔b5 followed by ...a4 wins for Black) **7...♔b5 8 ♗e8+ ♔c5 9 ♗d7** and Black cannot make progress. White always has a check if Black moves his king to b5 or c4, while otherwise Black is unable to support his pawns.

46) If Black is allowed to play ...♗d5 then he will have a perfect blockade. By giving up a pawn, White opens a path for his king to attack the a6-pawn: **1 d5! ♗xd5** (1...exd5 2 ♔d4 is similar) **2 ♔d4 ♔e7 3 ♔c5 ♗b7 4 ♔b6 ♗c8 5 ♔c7** (this manoeuvre drives the black bishop away and wins the a6-pawn, after which White's passed a-pawn will be decisive) **5...♗d7 6 ♔b7 e5 7 ♔xa6** (7 ♗xe5 is also good) **7...♔d6 8 ♔b7 ♗c6+ 9 ♔b8 ♔d5 10 a6 e4 11 a7 ♔c4 12 ♗e1** and White wins.

47) On an open board, a bishop is normally stronger than a knight. One danger is that the knight can be trapped, especially if it is on the edge of the board. Here White wins by **1 ♗e3!** (now the knight cannot move without being captured) **1...♔d7 2 ♔c5 ♔c7 3 d6+ ♔d7 4 ♔d5 ♔d8** (this would be the drawing move if it were just ♔+♙ vs ♔, but White can use his bishop to force a win) **5 ♔e6 ♔e8 6 d7+ ♔d8 7 ♗b6#.**

48) White can still win, but the bishop no longer controls the pawn's promotion square, so he must use a different method. **1 ♗e3!** (this is still the right first move, as White has no chance to win if the knight escapes) **1...♔e7 2 ♔d5 ♔d7 3 e6+ ♔e7 4 ♔e5 ♔e8** and now 5 ♔f6 ♔f8 6 e7+? ♔e8 only leads to a draw since 7 ♔e6 ♘g5+ 8 ♗xg5 is stalemate. Therefore White needs another idea: **5 ♔f5!** (the new plan is to take the trapped knight with the king) **5...♔e7 6 ♗c5+ ♔e8 7 ♔g4** and White picks up the knight with an easy win.

49) ♘+♙ vs ♗ is almost always a draw except if the pawn is far advanced, so White's winning chances appear slight. However, in this position a neat trick wins the enemy bishop. **1 ♔d2!** and amazingly the bishop is trapped, since **1...♗g4** and **1...♗h5** allow **2 ♘f6+** while **1...♗b3** and **1...♗a4** allow **2 ♘c5+**. The knight's ability to create forks proved decisive.

50) When holding up a pawn with a bishop, it's usually better for the bishop to occupy the longer of the two diagonals running through the square in front of the pawn. Here d8-h4 contains five squares, but d8-a5 only four. Although the position is symmetrical, which suggests that playing to one side is the same as playing to the other, Black only has one move to draw. **1...♗g5!** (1...♗a5? loses to 2 ♘c5 ♔c4 3 ♘b7 ♗b6 4 ♔c6 and White wins as the bishop has no safe squares on the d8-a5 diagonal) **2 ♘e5 ♔e4 3 ♘f7** (3 ♘c6, threatening ♘e7, is met by 3...♗f4+ 4 ♔e6 ♗c7, switching to the other diagonal; then the white king is too far away to run the bishop out of squares) **3...♗f6 4 ♔e6 ♗h4** and on this side of the board the extra square saves Black.

51) 1 ♗c4? is wrong since 1...♔d6! 2 ♗g8 ♔e7 3 ♗xh7 ♔f7 only leads to the bishop being lost after ...♔g7 (although in fact White can still draw). **1 ♔e5!** wins. Getting your king amongst the enemy pawns is decisive in most endings, as the king can often take one pawn after another: **1...♘d6 2 ♔f6 ♘c8** (2...♘e8+ 3 ♔f7 ♘d8 4 ♗g8 ♔e7 5 ♗xh7 ♔f7 6 ♗c4+ is also winning) **3 ♔g7 ♔d6 4 ♔xh7 ♘e7 5 ♔g7 ♔c7 6 ♔f6 ♔d6 7 ♗c4 ♔d7 8 ♗f7** and the remaining black pawns fall.

52) Black threatens ...f5, fixing the f4-pawn in place, and then ...♗d2 winning the pawn. White's first task is to prevent this. **1 f5! ♗d2** (both the white pawns are on light squares and cannot be attacked by the bishop, while Black's bishop is obstructed by the pawns on d6 and f6) **2 ♔c7** (White's plan is to play his king to c6 and knight to c8, when Black will lose the d-pawn) **2...♗a5+ 3 ♔c6 ♗d2 4 ♘c7 ♗f4 5 ♘a8 ♗e3 6 ♘b6 ♗f4** (6...♗xb6 7 ♔xb6 ♔d7 8 ♔b7 is also lost for Black) **7 ♘c8+ ♔d8 8 ♘xd6** and now White wins easily, for example by ♘e4, ♘c5, d6 and ♘e6+. As a rule, if you have just one bishop, you should **keep your pawns on squares not controlled by the bishop**, so they don't get in the bishop's way. In this position the knight was far superior to the bishop, which was unable to do anything useful.

53) White has a clear advantage because so many of Black's pawns are on light squares, obstructing the bishop, but if Black is allowed time to play ...♔e6 or ...♗d7 then White's pawns will be held back and his advantage much reduced. White should play **1 f5! f6** (the best chance; after 1...gxf5 2 ♘f4 Black cannot play 2...f6 due to 3 ♘xd5+ so White wins the h5-pawn, after which his own h-pawn will be decisive) **2 exf6+** (2 ♘f4 is also very good) **2...♔xf6 3 fxg6 ♗xg6** (3...♔xg6 4 ♘f4+ also costs Black a pawn) **4 ♘c3** and White wins a pawn at a4 or d5, which gives him a decisive advantage.

54) White is winning because the long-range bishop can support his own pawn while holding back the enemy b-pawn. Additionally, Black's knight is a long way from stopping the h-pawn. **1 h4** (1 ♗e6? is too slow and Black draws by 1...♘c7 2 ♗b3 ♔d6 3 h4 ♘e6+ 4 ♔f6 ♘f4) **1...b3** (1...♔d6 2 h5 ♔e7 3 h6 ♔f8 4 ♗e6 is another example of the white bishop serving two functions, since it prevents both ...♔g8 and ...b3, giving White time to play ♔g6 followed by h7) **2 h5 b2 3 ♗f5 ♘c7 4 h6 ♘e6+ 5 ♔f6 ♘f8 6 ♔e7!** and White wins. The bishop is preventing ...b1♕ while at the same time helping to trap the enemy knight.

55) It's wrong for White to promote too soon, since although 1 c8♕? ♘xc8 2 ♔xc8 wins the knight, it only leads to a draw. In order to win, White must do more than just win Black's knight for the c-pawn. 1 ♘c3? looks good as it threatens 2 ♘d5+, which would gain a queen when the c-pawn promotes. However, the surprising reply 1...♔e5! cuts out the knight check, after which Black has no trouble drawing. **1 ♘b4!** is correct, since it creates the double threat of 2 ♘d5+ and 2 ♘c6. Then **1...g4** (now 1...♔e5 may be met by 2 ♘c6+) **2 ♘d5+!** (2 ♘c6? g3 3 ♔xe7 g2 4 c8♕ g1♕ draws as ♕+♘ vs ♕ is generally drawn) **2...♘xd5 3 c8♕** gives White a decisive material advantage.

56) Black cannot save the game. It might look as if **1...♘d5** holds because 2 e8♕? ♘f6+ 3 ♔g5 ♘xe8 4 h5 ♘g7! 5 h6 ♘e6+ 6 ♔f6 ♘f8 is the draw of Exercise 9, but White wins with the surprising **2 e8♘!**, preventing the check on f6. Knights always struggle against rook's pawns, and here White's pieces are able to support the h-pawn's advance to the eighth rank: **2...♘e3+ 3 ♔g5 ♔e4 4 h5 ♘f5 5 ♔g6 ♘e7+** (after 5...♔e5 6 ♘g7 ♘e7+ 7 ♔f7 White wins at once) **6 ♔f6 ♘g8+ 7 ♔g7 ♘e7 8 ♘d6+** (not 8 h6? ♘f5+ followed by ...♘xh6) **8...♔e5 9 h6** and the pawn will promote.

57) White has a winning position. Both king and knight are short-range pieces, so find it hard to cope with widely separated passed pawns. Therefore the a- and h-pawns form a more dangerous combination than the d- and e-pawns. Play might continue **1 a6 ♘c6 2 ♘a2!** (other moves also win, but this is the simplest) **2...d5** (White also wins after 2...♔f5 3 ♘c3 followed by ♘xe4, and 2...♔f6 3 ♘b4 ♘a7 4 ♔e3) **3 ♘b4 ♘a7 4 ♘xd5!** and White wins. After **4...♔xd5 5 h6** Black cannot stop the h-pawn.

58) Breakthroughs are very important in opposite-coloured bishop endings and are often the only way to exploit an extra pawn (or two!). 1 e6? dxe6 2 b5 ♗d3! 3 b6 ♗a6 4 ♔e5 ♔f7 5 ♗b8 ♔e7 is only a draw, as is 1 ♔g5? ♔f7 followed by ...♔e6 with a blockade. The winning line is **1 b5! cxb5** (or 1...♗d3 2 bxc6 dxc6 3 e6 ♗c4 4 ♔e5 ♔g7 5 ♗e7 and Black's king is held back by the bishop and pawn, giving White time to play his king to d6: 5...♗a2 6 ♔d6 ♗c4 7 ♗h4 ♗d5 8 e7 ♔f7 9 ♔d7 ♗e6+ 10 ♔d8 and White wins) **2 e6! dxe6 3 c6** and the c-pawn cannot be stopped.

59) Since opposite-coloured bishops exert such a strong drawing tendency, the solution is sometimes to sacrifice your bishop! White must act at once; for example, 1 a5? ♗g7+ 2 ♔d3 ♔b7! (2...♗f8? allows the bishop sacrifice after all, and 3 ♗xd5! cxd5 4 ♔d4 wins as in the main line) 3 ♗e2 ♗f6 4 ♔e3 ♗e7 5 a6+ (it's perhaps surprising that getting both pawns to the sixth rank isn't enough to win) 5...♔b8 6 ♔d4 ♗f6+ 7 ♔d3 ♗e7 and White has to play ♔d4 again, repeating the position. Instead, **1 ♗xd5!** is the winning move, and after **1...cxd5** (1...♔b7 2 a5! ♗g7+ 3 ♔c4 doesn't help Black) **2 ♔xd5 ♔b7 3 a5** (the tidal wave of pawns overwhelms Black) **3...♗h6 4 c6+ ♔a6 5 c7 ♔b7 6 a6+** a pawn promotes.

60) 1 ♔e4? attempts to restrict the knight but gives Black time to bring his king in front of the pawn by 1...♔c7 2 f5 ♔d7 3 f6 ♔e6. 1 f5? is also bad, as it allows Black to eliminate the pawn and draw by 1...♘e3 2 f6 ♘g4+. White wins with **1 ♗f2!** (restricting the knight while keeping White's king in an active position) **1...♔c7** (the pawn also promotes after 1...♘b4 2 f5 ♘d3+ 3 ♔d4! ♘xf2 4 f6) **2 ♔e6!** (2 f5? ♔d7 3 f6 ♘b4! 4 ♗c5 ♘d3+ only draws; White must use his own king to shoulder away Black's) **2...♔d8 3 f5 ♔e8 4 f6 ♔f8 5 ♗c5+** and **6 f7+,** promoting the pawn. This exercise featured two key elements of playing with bishop against knight: using the bishop to restrict the knight and keeping an active king.

MAXIMUM CHECKING DISTANCE

4 Rook Endings

Rook endings occur more often than any other type of ending and are frequently misplayed, even by masters. Keeping a few important ideas in mind can avoid the mistakes that arise all too often in practical play.

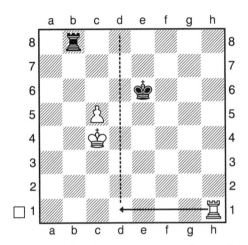
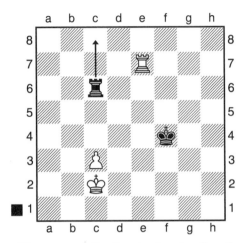

The rook has the power to control an entire file or rank, creating a barrier that the opposing king cannot cross. Here White wins by **1 ♖d1!**, which prevents Black's king from helping in the fight against the c-pawn. It turns out that Black's rook cannot cope with the pawn by itself. The winning line runs **1...♖c8** (or else White plays c6 followed by ♔c5) **2 ♔b5** (again threatening c6) **2...♖b8+ 3 ♔a6 ♖c8 4 ♔b6 ♖b8+ 5 ♔c7** (Black can no longer stop c6) **5...♖b2 6 c6 ♖c2 7 ♔b7 ♖b2+ 8 ♔c8 ♖c2 9 c7** with a standard winning position (see Exercise 25 on page 58). The important point here is the way you can use your rook to cut the enemy king off from the main battle.

If you are defending by bombarding the enemy king with checks, it helps to have the rook as far away from the opposing king as possible. White is threatening to win by **1 ♔b3 ♖b6+ 2 ♔a4 ♖c6 3 ♔b4 ♖b6+ 4 ♔c5** and now Black cannot prevent c4, which here leads to a win. The only move for Black to save the game is **1...♖c8!**, moving the rook as far as possible away from the enemy king. Now when the king emerges from behind the pawn to play c4, Black's checks are from longer range. After **2 ♔b3 ♖b8+ 3 ♔a4 ♖c8 4 ♔b4 ♖b8+ 5 ♔c5** (or 5 ♔a5 ♖c8 and the king must return to b4) **5...♖c8+ 6 ♔d4 ♖d8+** there is no way White can escape the harassment by the enemy rook except by returning with his king to c2. This idea is called the *principle of maximum checking distance*.

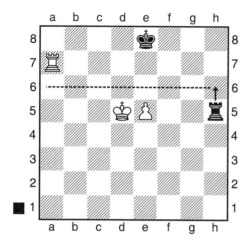

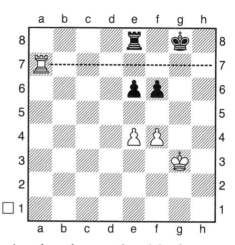

This should be a draw with Black to play, but positions of this type are often needlessly lost in practice. It looks bad for Black, as his king is cut off on the back rank and the white king and pawn are in an advanced position. Indeed, the natural 1...♖h1 2 ♔d6 ♖d1+? is wrong, since White can win by 3 ♔e6 ♔d8 4 ♖a8+ ♔c7 5 ♔f6 and the e-pawn will advance. This line wins because White's king can shelter from checks on e6.

Nevertheless, there's a simple plan of defence that enables Black to draw. He plays **1...♖h6!** to prevent the white king from advancing any further. After **2 e6** (intending 3 ♔d6) **2...♖h1!** Black is ready to give checks from the back rank. The white king no longer has any shelter since e6 is occupied by the pawn, and after **3 ♔d6 ♖d1+ 4 ♔e5 ♖e1+ 5 ♔f6 ♖f1+** White cannot win. The key point was the way the black rook set up a barrier along its third rank, and for that reason this idea is called the *third-rank defence*.

A rook on the seventh rank is often a major asset, especially in two cases. The first is when there are several enemy pawns on the seventh rank that can be attacked by the rook. The second is when the opposing king is cut off on the back rank. That's the case here, but to win White needs to bring his own king into the attack. **1 ♔h4!** (not 1 ♔g4?, when Black draws by 1...f5+! 2 exf5 exf5+ 3 ♔xf5 ♖b8 4 ♔g5 ♖b6 with the third-rank defence from the previous position) **1...♖b8** (now 1...f5 can be met by 2 e5 followed by ♔g5) **2 ♔h5 ♖b4** (2...♖c8 3 ♔g6 ♖f8 4 ♖g7+ ♔h8 5 ♖f7 is hopeless for Black) **3 ♔g6** (an active king is very important in rook endings; now White is threatening mate by ♖a8+) **3...♔f8 4 ♔xf6 ♔e8 5 ♖e7+ ♔f8 6 ♖xe6** and White wins easily with his two extra pawns.

53

Exercises

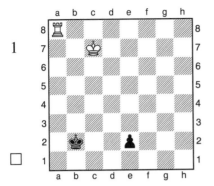

1

Can you find the only move to win for White?

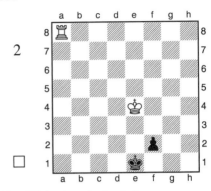

2

Can White (to play) win?

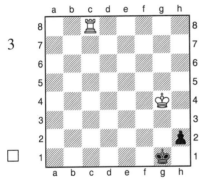

3

This is the previous exercise shifted two files to the right. Can White win now?

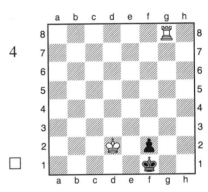

4

Which move wins for White?

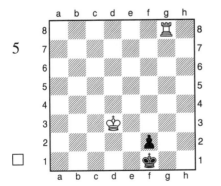

5

White's king is now on d3 instead of d2. Can he win here?

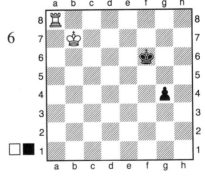

6

If White is to play, how does he win? What is the result with Black to move?

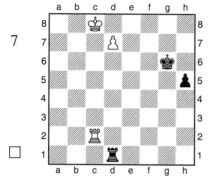

7

Should White play 1 d8♛, 1 ♖c5 or 1 ♖c4?

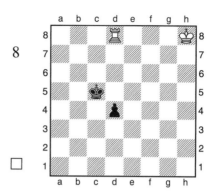

8

Is this a win for White?

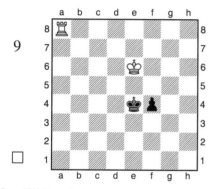

9

Can White win?

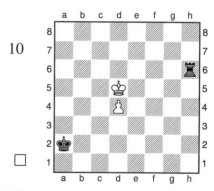

10

White should move his king to clear the way for the pawn. Is 1 ♔c5 or 1 ♔e5 correct?

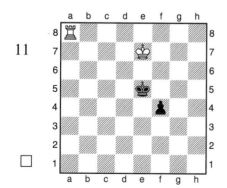

11

Should White use his rook from the side by 1 ♖a5+, or from behind with 1 ♖f8?

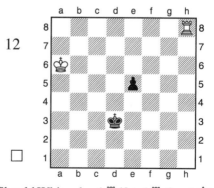

12

Should White play 1 ♖d8+, 1 ♖e8 or 1 ♔b5?

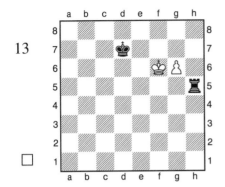

13

What is the result if White is to play?

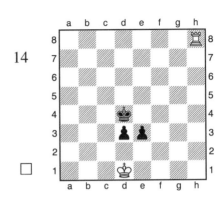

14

Can White win against Black's far-advanced pawns?

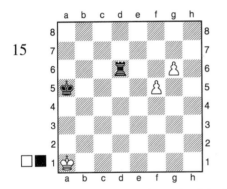

15

What is the result if White is to play? And if Black is to play?

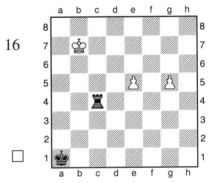

16

Which pawn should White push?

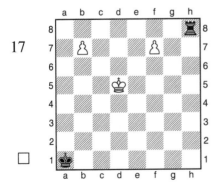

17

Can White win?

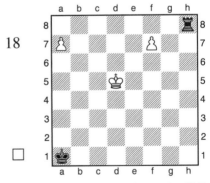

18

Now the pawn is on a7 instead of b7. Can White win now?

56

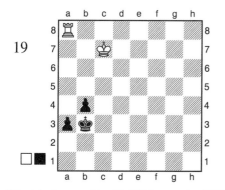

19

What is the result with White to play? With Black to play?

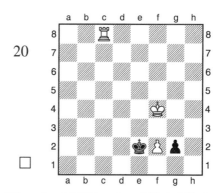

20

What should White play: 1 ♖c1, 1 ♖c2+ or 1 ♖g8?

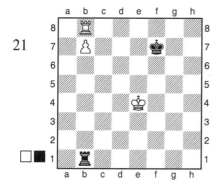

21

What is the result with White to play? With Black to play?

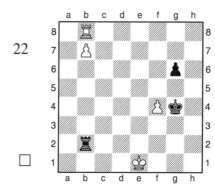

22

Which move wins for White?

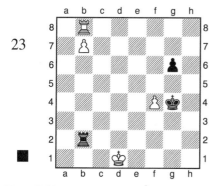

23

Here White has played 1 ♔d1? in the position from the previous exercise. How does Black now draw?

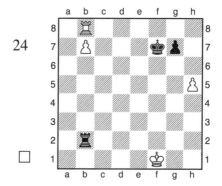

24

White had the idea to play 1 h6 gxh6 2 ♖h8 ♖xb7 3 ♖h7+. Does 1 h6 win?

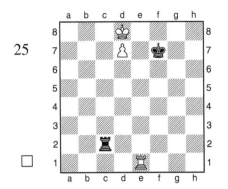

25

White's pawn is one square from queening, but his king is blocking it. Can he win?

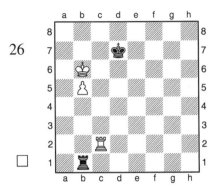

26

Here the pawn is further back. Can White win now?

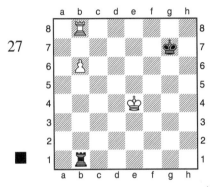

27

Compared to Exercise 21 (after 1...♔g7), the pawn is now on b6 rather than b7. If Black is to play, what is the result?

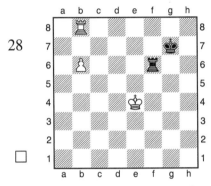

28

Here Black is attacking the pawn from the side. Can White win?

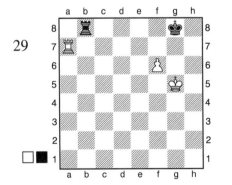

29

What is the result with White to play? With Black to play?

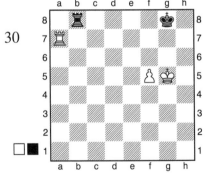

30

Now the pawn is on f5 rather than f6. Does this make a difference with White to play? With Black to play?

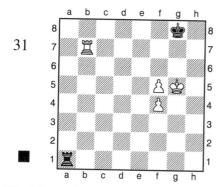

31

Black has only one move to draw. Can you find it?

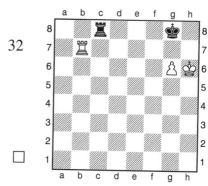

32

The same as Exercise 29 (after 1 ♔g6) but shifted one file to the right. Can White win now?

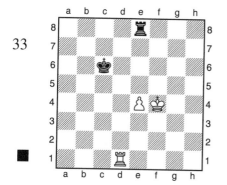

33

White is threatening to play e5. Is there any defence for Black?

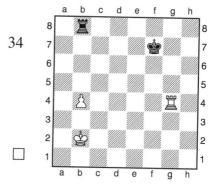

34

Is the best move 1 ♔b3, intending ♔c4 (or ♔a4) and b5, or 1 ♖e4, preventing the enemy king from approaching the pawn?

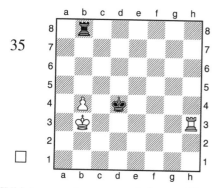

35

Which move is correct: 1 ♔a4, 1 ♖c3 or 1 ♖h5?

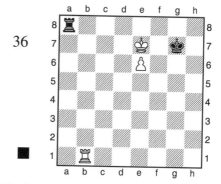

36

Find the only drawing move for Black.

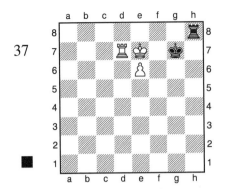

37

Which is the best move: 1...♔g6, 1...♖a8 or 1...♖b8?

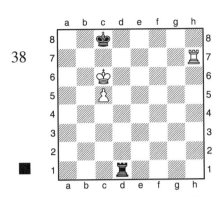

38

White threatens to win with 1 ♖h8+, so Black must move his king. Should he play 1...♔d8 or 1...♔b8?

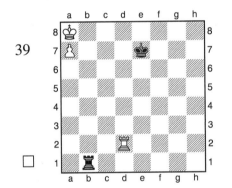

39

This is similar to Exercise 25, except that White has an a-pawn. Can he win?

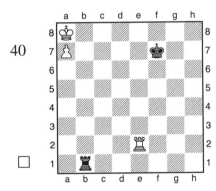

40

Here Black's king is further away. Can White win now?

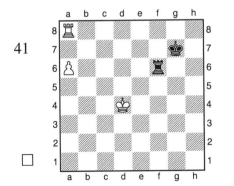

41

This is Exercise 27 with the pawn shifted to the a-file. Is it still a win?

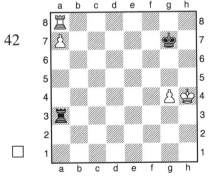

42

Can White win?

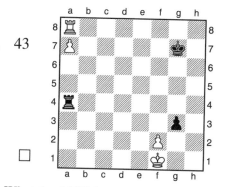

43

What should White play here: 1 fxg3, 1 f3 or 1 f4?

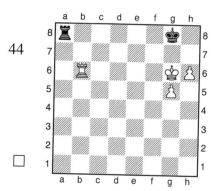

44

White played 1 h7+. Was this a good move?

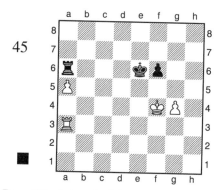

45

Does Black (to play) lose here?

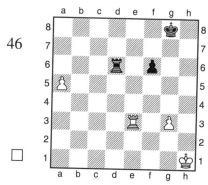

46

Which move is correct: 1 ♖a3, 1 ♔g2 or 1 ♖e8+?

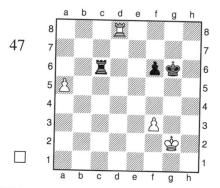

47

White has only one move to win. Can you find it?

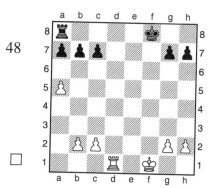

48

Which move is best for White?

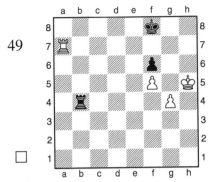

49

Which is the winning move for White?

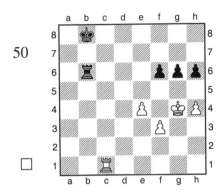

50

Find the best move for White.

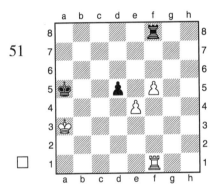

51

Should White play 1 exd5 or 1 e5?

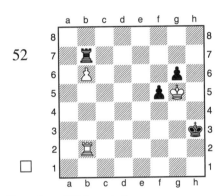

52

How does White win?

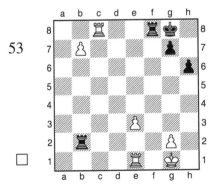

53

How can White win by making use of his far-advanced pawn?

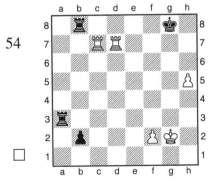

54

Is the correct result a win for White, a draw or a win for Black?

Tougher Exercises

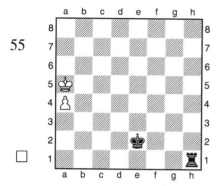

55

What would you play here, 1 ♔b4, 1 ♔b5 or 1 ♔b6?

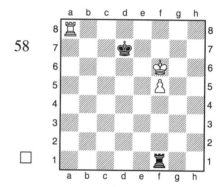

56

How does Black draw?

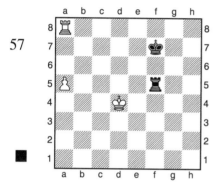

57

Bearing in mind Exercise 41, what should Black play here: 1...♔e7 or 1...♔g7?

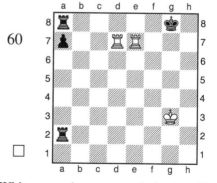

58

Is the right plan 1 ♔g6 followed by f6 and ♔f7, 1 ♖a5 followed by ♔f7 and f6, or 1 ♖f8 followed by ♔g7 and f6?

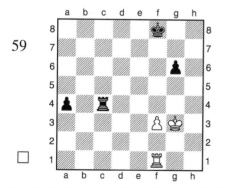

59

Should White play 1 f4, 1 ♖b1 or 1 ♖h1?

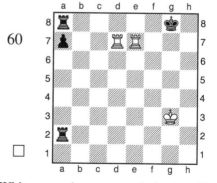

60

White can give perpetual check with his rooks, but can he win?

Solutions to Rook Endings Exercises

1) **1 罝e8!** wins the pawn, since the black king is too far away to defend it. 1 罝b8+? only chases Black's king nearer the pawn, and after 1...♔c2 2 罝e8 ♔d2 White cannot win.

2) White cannot win. The best he can do is **1 罝a1+ ♔e2 2 罝a2+ ♔e1 3 ♔e3**. Then 3...f1♕? is met by 4 罝a1#, but **3...f1♘+!** saves the game as the ending of 罝 vs ♘ is generally drawn. There are winning positions when the defender's king is stuck on the edge of the board, but this is not one of them. We shall consider this type of position in more detail later (Exercise 19 on page 77).

3) Now it is a win for White. After **1 ♔g3!** Black must again promote to a knight, but this time **1...h1♘+** (1...h1♕ 2 罝c1#) **2 ♔f3** leaves the knight stuck in the corner. Then **2...♔h2** (2...♘f2 3 罝c1+ ♔h2 4 ♔xf2 is also winning for White) **3 罝g8** wins for White as Black must give up his knight to avoid immediate mate.

4) **1 罝f8! ♔g2 2 ♔e2** wins the black pawn and is the only way to win. 1 ♔d1? is wrong as Black is stalemated, and 1 ♔e3? ♔e1 2 罝a8 fails because of 2...f1♘+!, as in Exercise 2.

5) White cannot win. After **1 罝f8** (1 ♔d2 is stalemate, and 1 ♔e3 is a draw as in the previous exercise) **1...♔e1! 2 罝e8+** (or else Black promotes) **2...♔d1 3 罝f8 ♔e1** White is only repeating the position.

6) If White is to play he wins by **1 罝a5!**, creating a barrier that prevents Black's king from supporting the pawn. After **1...♔g6** (1...g3 2 罝a3 g2 3 罝g3 and White wins the pawn) **2 ♔c6 ♔f6 3 ♔d6 ♔g6 4 罝e5** followed by ♔d5 and ♔e4 the pawn will soon fall. This idea is called the *fifth-rank cut-off*. With Black to play, **1...♔f5** (1...g3? loses to 2 罝a3 g2 3 罝g3) draws, as the king can now usher the pawn forward. After **2 ♔c6 g3 3 ♔d5 ♔f4 4 ♔d4 g2 5 罝g8 ♔f3 6 ♔d3 ♔f2 7 罝f8+ ♔e1 8 罝g8 ♔f2** White cannot win.

7) White must not rush to win the rook since 1 d8♕? 罝xd8+ 2 ♔xd8 ♔g5! (2...h4? loses to 3 罝c5!) 3 ♔e7 h4 4 ♔e6 h3 5 ♔e5 ♔g4 6 ♔e4 ♔g3 7 ♔e3 h2 8 罝c1 ♔g2 is only a draw. 1 罝c4? ♔g5 is also bad as it just helps Black by giving him a free move. The winning move is **1 罝c5!**, in order to establish a fifth-rank cut-off as in Exercise 6. After **1...h4 2 d8♕ 罝xd8+ 3 ♔xd8** White wins, as **3...h3** loses the pawn to **4 罝c3 h2 5 罝h3**, while otherwise Black can only wait while White brings his king back and eventually wins Black's pawn.

8) Black's king is supporting his pawn and to win White needs to use his own king. **1 ♔g7!** (White's king must take the shortest route to attack the enemy pawn) **1...♔c4 2 ♔f6 d3 3 ♔e5 ♔c3 4 ♔e4 d2 5 ♔e3** and the pawn falls.

9) White cannot win. He can chase the enemy pieces up the board, but he cannot do better than reach the draw of Exercise 2 after **1 罝a4+ ♔e3 2 ♔e5** (or 2 ♔f5 f3 3 ♔g4 f2 4 罝a1 ♔e2, also with a draw) **2...f3 3 罝a3+ ♔e2 4 ♔e4 f2 5 罝a2+ ♔e1 6 ♔e3 f1♘+**. It follows that if this position is shifted two files to the right, so that Black's pawn is on the h-file, then White wins because the same manoeuvre leads to the win of Exercise 3.

10) As well as advancing his own pawn, White must shoulder away Black's king. Thus the white king must move to the same side of the pawn as Black's king: **1 ♔c5!** (1 ♔c4! also draws) **1...♔b3 2 d5 ♔a4 3 d6** draws easily, but 1 ♔e5? ♔b3 2 d5 ♔c4 3 d6 ♔c5 4 d7 罝d6 loses.

11) The rook should operate from behind. 1 罝a5+? ♔e4 2 ♔e6 f3 3 罝a4+ ♔e3 4 ♔e5 f2 5 罝a1 ♔e2 is only a draw, but **1 罝f8! ♔e4 2 ♔f6!** (the key idea is for White to switch his king to the g-file, so that he can attack the pawn without being obstructed by Black's king) **2...f3 3 ♔g5 ♔e3 4 ♔g4 f2 5 ♔g3** leads to the capture of Black's pawn.

12) White only draws after 1 ♖e8? e4 2 ♔b5 e3 3 ♔b4 e2 4 ♔b3 ♔d2 5 ♖d8+ ♔c1 or 1 ♔b5? e4 2 ♔b4 e3 3 ♔b3 e2. The sole way to win is **1 ♖d8+!** (playing an *in-between check* gains a move for White) **1...♔c3** (or 1...♔e3 2 ♔b5 e4 3 ♔c4 ♔f2 4 ♖e8 e3 5 ♔d3) **2 ♖e8** (the point of the check is that Black cannot immediately push his pawn) **2...♔d4** (White has transferred his rook from h8 to e8, effectively gaining a move) **3 ♔b5 e4 4 ♔b4 e3 5 ♔b3 ♔d3 6 ♖d8+ ♔e2 7 ♔c2 ♔f2 8 ♖e8 e2 9 ♔d2** and White wins.

13) On rare occasions, it can happen that a far-advanced pawn beats a rook. Here White can promote his pawn and win by **1 g7 ♖h6+ 2 ♔f5!** (Black draws after both 2 ♔f7? ♖h7 followed by ...♖xg7, and 2 ♔g5? ♖h1, when White must play 3 ♔f6 or 3 ♔g6 even to draw, since 3 g8♕? loses to 3...♖g1+) **2...♖h5+ 3 ♔f4** (3 ♔g4?? ♖h1 is winning for Black) **3...♖h4+ 4 ♔f3** (4 ♔g3 ♖h1 5 ♔g2 is equally good) **4...♖h3+ 5 ♔g2** and the pawn promotes, leading to the winning ending of ♕ vs ♖ (see Exercise 19 on page 87).

14) If the side with the rook has his king in front of two connected pawns, the rook almost always wins no matter how far advanced the pawns are. Here the simplest method is **1 ♖e8** (now Black must push a pawn or he loses the e3-pawn at once) **1...e2+** (or 1...d2 2 ♔e2 ♔c3 3 ♖xe3+ ♔c2 4 ♔d3) **2 ♔d2 ♔c4 3 ♖e4+ ♔d5 4 ♖xd3** and both pawns fall.

15) If White is to play then he wins by **1 g7! ♖d1+ 2 ♔b2 ♖g1 3 f6** followed by f7, promoting one of the pawns and leading to ♕ vs ♖. If Black is to play, he wins due to his extra move: **1...♖d1+! 2 ♔b2 ♖g1** (this stops both pawns from advancing and a subsequent ...♖g5 will win them) **3 ♔c3 ♖g5 4 ♔d4 ♖xf5 5 ♔e4 ♖g5**, winning the other pawn. Two connected passed pawns far away from the enemy king generally win against a rook if both can reach the sixth rank or (as here) one can reach the seventh while the other is on the fifth.

16) Pushing the g-pawn is correct, because Black's rook will be forced to take it, when White's king will be close enough to support the remaining pawn: **1 g6! ♖g4 2 ♔c7 ♖xg6 3 ♔d7 ♔b2 4 e6** with an easy draw. Doing it the other way around loses both pawns: 1 e6? ♖e4 2 g6 ♖xe6 3 g7 ♖g6 and Black wins.

17) White can win with **1 ♔d6** threatening 2 ♔e7 followed by f8♕. Black can only meet this by **1...♖b8** (to answer 2 ♔e7? with 2...♖xb7+), but then **2 ♔c7 ♖f8 3 b8♕ ♖xf7+** leads to the winning ending of ♕ vs ♖.

18) The extra file between the pawns guarantees a draw. After **1 ♔d6** White again threatens 2 ♔e7, but now **1...♖a8!** is a good defence. Then 2 ♔e7 ♖xa7+ draws as before, while **2 ♔c6** (threatening 3 ♔b7) is met by **2...♖f8** and White cannot make progress. When White threatens to support one pawn with his king, Black switches his rook in front of the other.

19) White, to play, can draw by attacking the rear pawn with his king: **1 ♔b6 ♔b2 2 ♔b5 b3 3 ♔b4 a2 4 ♖a7 a1♕** (there is nothing better) **5 ♖xa1 ♔xa1 6 ♔xb3**. If Black is to play, he wins with the clever idea **1...♔a2!** (the b-pawn is the dangerous one, because the white rook is not currently behind it; not 1...a2? 2 ♔b6 ♔b2 3 ♔b5 b3 4 ♔b4 with a draw as in the White-to-play line) **2 ♔b6 b3 3 ♔a5 b2 4 ♖b8 b1♕ 5 ♖xb1 ♔xb1** and White is one move too slow.

20) An ending with ♖+♙ vs ♙ is usually an easy win, since if the enemy pawn becomes dangerous you can almost always give up the rook for the pawn and win with your own pawn, but occasionally you must take care. Here 1 ♖g8? ♔xf2 draws at once, while 1 ♖c1? ♔xf2 2 ♖c2+ is a draw after 2...♔g1 (the simplest, but even 2...♔f1 3 ♔f3 g1♘+ draws) 3 ♔g3 ♔h1 4 ♖xg2 stalemate. The winning line is **1 ♖c2+! ♔d1** (1...♔d3 loses to 2 ♖c1 ♔e2 3 ♔g3) **2 ♖a2! g1♕** (2...♔e1 3 ♔e3) **3 ♖a1+** and White wins the queen with a skewer.

21) White wins by **1 ♖h8!** (threatening 2 b8♕) **1...♖xb7 2 ♖h7+**, a tactic important in many rook endings. If Black is to play, he draws with **1...♔g7**, preventing the above tactic. So long as Black keeps his king on g7 or h7 White cannot win. If White approaches the b7-pawn with his king, Black just checks him away; for example, **2 ♔d5 ♔h7 3 ♔c6 ♖c1+ 4 ♔d7 ♖d1+** and so on.

22) The key idea is to move the rook from b8 with check, gaining time to promote the b7-pawn. White can achieve this with a pawn sacrifice opening a file: **1 f5!** and after **1...♔xf5 2 ♖f8+** or **1...gxf5 2 ♖g8+** White wins Black's rook. **1...g5** avoids a rook check, but after **2 f6** Black cannot stop both white pawns.

23) White is still threatening to play f5, so Black must first neutralize this threat. The only move to achieve this is **1...♔f3!** so that Black can answer f5 by ...gxf5 without allowing a rook check. The only other try for White is to attack the g-pawn with his king, but this doesn't work if Black defends correctly: **2 ♔c1 ♖b6 3 ♔c2 ♖b5 4 ♔c3 ♖b6 5 ♔d4 ♖b1 6 ♔e5 ♖b6!** and White cannot make progress since 7 f5 loses a pawn after 7...♖b5+.

24) **1 h6** doesn't win, but as the position is a draw in any case it's worth a try, especially as the defence is not at all obvious. Black's only way out is **1...♔g6! 2 ♔e1** (2 hxg7 ♔xg7 puts the black king in the safe zone of g7 and h7) **2...♔h7** (Black still can't take the h-pawn, as both 2...gxh6? 3 ♖g8+ and 2...♔xh6? 3 ♖h8+ win for White, but now he is genuinely threatening ...gxh6) **3 hxg7** (there's not much choice) **3...♔xg7** and the danger is over.

25) This winning situation (white pawn on b7, c7, d7, e7, f7 or g7, white king in front, black rook attacking from behind) is extremely important because a great many rook endings eventually reduce to it. This whole family of positions is collectively known as the *Lucena position*. In the diagram there are even two ways for White to win. The first is to play White's rook to c8, forcing the black rook off the c-file: **1 ♖a1 ♖c3 2 ♖a8 ♖c2 3 ♖c8 ♖a2 4 ♔c7 ♖c2+ 5 ♔b6 ♖b2+ 6 ♔a5 ♖a2+ 7 ♔b4 ♖b2+ 8 ♔a3** and White wins. The second is slightly trickier but works even when the first method doesn't (this is the case if White has a b-pawn or a g-pawn): **1 ♖f1+ ♔g7 2 ♖f4!** (the point of this odd-looking move will be clear later) **2...♖c1 3 ♔e7 ♖e1+ 4 ♔d6 ♖d1+ 5 ♔e6 ♖e1+** (or 5...♔g6 6 ♖f8 ♖e1+ 7 ♔d6 ♖d1+ 8 ♔c6 ♖c1+ 9 ♔b5 ♖b1+ 10 ♔a4 ♖a1+ 11 ♔b3 ♖b1+ 12 ♔a2) **6 ♔d5 ♖d1+ 7 ♖d4** and the point of playing ♖f4 is revealed, since White can now promote his pawn. The second method is called *building a bridge*.

26) White wins because Black cannot avoid reaching the previous exercise; for example, **1 ♔a6 ♖a1+ 2 ♔b7 ♖b1 3 b6 ♖b3 4 ♔a7 ♖a3+ 5 ♔b8 ♖b3 6 b7 ♖a3 7 ♖d2+ ♔e7 8 ♖d4!** and then as in the second method given in Exercise 25 (necessary here as White has a b-pawn).

27) Surprisingly, having the pawn one square further back helps White as Black's checking defence no longer works. The result is that White wins: **1...♖b5** (1...♔f7 2 ♔d5 ♔e7 3 ♔c6 is similar) **2 ♔d4 ♔f7 3 ♔c4 ♖b1 4 ♔c5 ♖c1+ 5 ♔d6 ♖d1+ 6 ♔c7 ♖c1+ 7 ♔b7** (this is where White takes advantage of the pawn's position on b6 as opposed to b7) **7...♔e7 8 ♖h8**

(there's nothing Black can do to prevent White from reaching the Lucena position) **8...♔d7 9 ♔b8 ♖b1 10 b7 ♖a1 11 ♖h4** and so on, as in Exercise 25.

28) White can win by supporting the pawn with his king: **1 ♔d5 ♖f5+ 2 ♔c6 ♖f6+ 3 ♔b5 ♖f5+ 4 ♔a6** (it's important that White is able to shelter from the checks by playing his king to the left of the pawn) **4...♖f6 5 ♔a7 ♖f1 6 ♖e8 ♔f7 7 ♖e2** with an easy win.

29) If it is White's move, he wins by **1 ♔g6**, trapping Black's rook on the back rank due to the possibility of ♖a8+. After **1...♖c8 2 ♔g7+ ♔f8** (or 2...♔h8 3 ♖h7+ ♔g8 4 f7+ ♔f8 5 ♖h8+) **3 ♖h7!** (threatening ♖h8#) **3...♔g8 4 f7+ ♔f8 5 ♖h8+** White wins the rook. If Black is to play, he draws by checking with his rook from behind the pawn: **1...♖b1 2 ♔g6 ♖g1+ 3 ♔f5 ♖f1+ 4 ♔e6 ♖e1+** and Black just keeps checking. If White tries **5 ♔d7** then **5...♔f7** wins the pawn, but not 5...♖d1+? 6 ♔e8 ♖e1+ 7 ♖e7, when White wins.

30) Surprisingly, it doesn't make a difference in either case. If White is to play, he can still confine Black's rook to the back rank with **1 ♔g6**. Then he plays **2 f6**, winning as in the previous exercise. If it is Black's move, he can draw using the *third-rank defence*, which was described in the left-hand diagram on page 53. If there is one thing you should know about rook endings, it is this defence. The key move is **1...♖b6**, preventing the white king from advancing. Then Black waits until White pushes his f-pawn, when he plays his rook to its eighth rank: **2 f6 ♖b1 3 ♔g6 ♖g1+**, drawing as in the previous exercise.

31) The third-rank defence also works well when White has an extra doubled pawn, although Black must be a little more careful. The drawing line runs **1...♖a6!** (any other move allows White to win) **2 f6** (2 ♖e7 ♔f8 3 ♖e6 is another try, but 3...♖a7 4 ♔f6 ♖f7+ 5 ♔g6 ♖g7+ defends) **2...♖a1** (the same idea as with a single pawn: now that f6 is blocked, Black switches to checking from behind) **3 ♔g6 ♖g1+! 4 ♔f5 ♔f8 5 ♔e6 ♖e1+** and Black draws, as he can always meet ♔e6 by ...♖e1+ and ♔g6 with ...♖g1+.

32) Now the position is a draw because there's no room for the winning idea from Exercise 29. After **1 ♖g7+ ♔h8 2 ♖h7+ ♔g8** White would like to play his rook one square to the right, but that would be off the edge of the board! There's no other winning attempt for White (3 g7?? would even lose after 3...♖c6+) so it's a draw.

33) White intends e5, after which he will be able to advance his king and head for the Lucena position. If Black can prevent this he will draw, and the correct method is **1...♖f8+ 2 ♔g5 ♖e8!** (2...♖g8+? loses to 3 ♔f6 ♖f8+ 4 ♔e7 followed by e5) **3 ♔f5 ♖f8+ 4 ♔e6** (or 4 ♔g6 ♖e8) **4...♖e8+** and White must go back. Black can always stop the pawn's advance by checking or attacking the e-pawn, depending on the position of the white king.

34) When the enemy king is not in front of the pawn, it's often possible to use your rook to cut the king off permanently. White only draws after 1 ♔b3? ♔e6! (not 1...♔e7? 2 ♖d4 ♔e6 3 ♔c4 ♖c8+ 4 ♔b5 ♖b8+ 5 ♔c6, when White wins as the rook defends the pawn) 2 ♖d4 ♔e5! (driving the rook away from d4, its best square) 3 ♖d1 ♔e6 4 ♔c4 ♖c8+ 5 ♔b5 ♖b8+ 6 ♔c5 ♖c8+ 7 ♔b6 ♖b8+ and the king must go back, so cutting the king off with the rook along the d-file is not good enough. Instead **1 ♖e4!** is the winning move. Then **1...♔f6 2 ♔b3 ♔f5 3 ♖e1 ♔f6 4 ♔c4 ♖c8+ 5 ♔d5 ♖b8 6 ♔c5 ♖c8+ 7 ♔d6 ♖b8** (Black tries the drawing method of the previous exercise, but it doesn't work here because his king is too far away) **8 ♖f1+** (nudging the king a little further away) **8...♔g6 9 ♖b1 ♔f7 10 b5 ♔e8 11 ♔c7**

Ξa8 12 b6 is winning for White. The basic rule is that **you should cut the enemy king off as far away from the pawn as possible**.

35) 1 Ξc3? $\dot{\mbox{$\Phi$}}$d5 2 $\dot{\mbox{$\Phi$}}$a4 Ξa8+ 3 $\dot{\mbox{$\Phi$}}$b5 Ξb8+ 4 $\dot{\mbox{$\Phi$}}$a5 Ξa8+ 5 $\dot{\mbox{$\Phi$}}$b6 Ξb8+ and 1 $\dot{\mbox{$\Phi$}}$a4? Ξa8+ 2 $\dot{\mbox{$\Phi$}}$b5 Ξb8+ 3 $\dot{\mbox{$\Phi$}}$a5 Ξa8+ 4 $\dot{\mbox{$\Phi$}}$b6 Ξb8+ both lead to nothing. Instead **1 Ξh5!** is the winning move. This cuts the black king off along the fifth rank. Black can no longer bring his king back and cannot prevent White from edging his pawn forwards: **1...Ξc8 2 b5 Ξc5** (2...Ξb8 3 $\dot{\mbox{$\Phi$}}$b4 followed by Ξh6 and b6 allows White to keep nudging his pawn up the board) **3 Ξh4+** (3 Ξxc5? $\dot{\mbox{$\Phi$}}$xc5 4 $\dot{\mbox{$\Phi$}}$a4 $\dot{\mbox{$\Phi$}}$b6 is a draw) **3...$\dot{\mbox{$\Phi$}}$d5 4 $\dot{\mbox{$\Phi$}}$b4 Ξc1 5 $\dot{\mbox{$\Phi$}}$a5 Ξa1+ 6 $\dot{\mbox{$\Phi$}}$b6** and White will soon reach the Lucena position. Cutting the king off along a rank is generally even more effective than cutting it off along a file.

36) Black must check immediately. Any delay would allow White to drive Black's king away by Ξg1+, and then White can reach the Lucena position. The drawing line is **1...Ξa7+! 2 $\dot{\mbox{$\Phi$}}$d6 Ξa6+ 3 $\dot{\mbox{$\Phi$}}$d7 Ξa7+ 4 $\dot{\mbox{$\Phi$}}$c8 Ξa8+** (to escape the checks, the white king must go all the way to the b-file, and then Black can win the white pawn) **5 $\dot{\mbox{$\Phi$}}$b7 Ξe8 6 Ξe1 $\dot{\mbox{$\Phi$}}$f6** and the pawn falls.

37) 1...$\dot{\mbox{$\Phi$}}$g6? quickly leads to the Lucena position after 2 Ξd8 Ξh1 3 $\dot{\mbox{$\Phi$}}$d7, while 1...Ξb8? loses to 2 Ξd8 Ξb7+ 3 $\dot{\mbox{$\Phi$}}$d6 Ξb6+ 4 $\dot{\mbox{$\Phi$}}$d7 Ξb7+ 5 $\dot{\mbox{$\Phi$}}$c6 Ξe7 (if the rook moves along the file, White just plays e7) 6 $\dot{\mbox{$\Phi$}}$d6. There is only one way to draw, **1...Ξa8!** (the difference between this and 1...Ξb8? is subtle but important) **2 Ξd8 Ξa7+ 3 $\dot{\mbox{$\Phi$}}$d6 Ξa6+ 4 $\dot{\mbox{$\Phi$}}$d7 Ξa7+ 5 $\dot{\mbox{$\Phi$}}$c6 Ξa6+** and White cannot stop the checks. Here it's possible to find the correct move using the *principle of maximum checking distance*, described on page 52. Checking from the b-file loses but using the rook on the a-file is enough to draw.

38) 1...$\dot{\mbox{$\Phi$}}$d8? loses to 2 Ξh8+ $\dot{\mbox{$\Phi$}}$e7 3 $\dot{\mbox{$\Phi$}}$c7 as Black cannot prevent the Lucena position, but **1...$\dot{\mbox{$\Phi$}}$b8!** draws. After **2 Ξh8+ $\dot{\mbox{$\Phi$}}$a7 3 $\dot{\mbox{$\Phi$}}$c7 Ξg1!** (3...Ξf1 also draws) **4 Ξh7** (4 c6 Ξg7+ is a draw after 5 $\dot{\mbox{$\Phi$}}$d6 Ξg6+ 6 $\dot{\mbox{$\Phi$}}$d7 Ξg7+ or 5 $\dot{\mbox{$\Phi$}}$c8 $\dot{\mbox{$\Phi$}}$b6 6 Ξh6 Ξc7+ winning the pawn) **4...Ξg8 5 c6 $\dot{\mbox{$\Phi$}}$a6** Black draws, since if White's rook leaves the seventh rank Black starts checking.

39) White cannot win. There's no equivalent to the Lucena position with a rook's pawn, and positions with the king stuck in front are drawn, except if the defender's king is far away. Here White can only try playing his rook round to b8, but it does not win: **1 Ξh2 $\dot{\mbox{$\Phi$}}$d7 2 Ξh8 $\dot{\mbox{$\Phi$}}$c7 3 Ξb8 Ξh1 4 Ξb7+ $\dot{\mbox{$\Phi$}}$c6 5 Ξb2 Ξh8+ 6 Ξb8 Ξh1** and White is not getting anywhere. The difference compared to a b-pawn is that the edge of the board prevents the white king from moving to the left of the pawn.

40) White can win if Black's king is far enough away from the pawn, although it is quite tricky. Here the win runs **1 Ξh2 $\dot{\mbox{$\Phi$}}$e7 2 Ξh8 $\dot{\mbox{$\Phi$}}$d6** (2...$\dot{\mbox{$\Phi$}}$d7 3 Ξb8 Ξa1 4 $\dot{\mbox{$\Phi$}}$b7 Ξb1+ 5 $\dot{\mbox{$\Phi$}}$a6 Ξa1+ 6 $\dot{\mbox{$\Phi$}}$b6 Ξb1+ 7 $\dot{\mbox{$\Phi$}}$c5 Ξc1+ 8 $\dot{\mbox{$\Phi$}}$d4 Ξd1+ 9 $\dot{\mbox{$\Phi$}}$c3 Ξc1+ 10 $\dot{\mbox{$\Phi$}}$d2 is also winning) **3 Ξb8 Ξa1 4 $\dot{\mbox{$\Phi$}}$b7 Ξb1+ 5 $\dot{\mbox{$\Phi$}}$c8** (5 $\dot{\mbox{$\Phi$}}$a6 only wastes time as the king cannot escape down the board when Black's king is on d6: 5...Ξa1+ 6 $\dot{\mbox{$\Phi$}}$b6 Ξb1+, etc.) **5...Ξc1+ 6 $\dot{\mbox{$\Phi$}}$d8 Ξh1** (threatening mate) **7 Ξb6+ $\dot{\mbox{$\Phi$}}$c5 8 Ξc6+!** (an important point which isn't easy to spot if you don't know it) **8...$\dot{\mbox{$\Phi$}}$d5** (after 8...$\dot{\mbox{$\Phi$}}$xc6 9 a8$\mbox{$\mathbb{W}$}$+ White promotes with check and wins the black rook) **9 Ξa6 Ξh8+ 10 $\dot{\mbox{$\Phi$}}$c7 Ξh7+ 11 $\dot{\mbox{$\Phi$}}$b6 Ξh6+ 12 $\dot{\mbox{$\Phi$}}$a5** and White finally wins.

41) This position is a draw. Rook's pawns offer more drawing chances than other pawns because White's king has no space to the left of the pawn. White can only try **1 $\dot{\mbox{$\Phi$}}$c5** but then Black draws by sideways checks: **1...Ξf5+ 2 $\dot{\mbox{$\Phi$}}$b6 Ξf6+ 3 $\dot{\mbox{$\Phi$}}$b7 Ξf7+** and there is no shelter from the checks. The sideways check defence only works against a rook's pawn, but then it can be very effective.

42) Even though White is two pawns ahead, the position is a draw. After **1 ♔g5** (1 g5 ♖a4+ 2 ♔g3 ♖a3+ 3 ♔f4 ♖a4+ 4 ♔e5 ♖a5+ 5 ♔d6 ♖a6+ is similar) **1...♖a5+ 2 ♔f4 ♖a4+ 3 ♔e5 ♖a5+ 4 ♔d6 ♖a6+ 5 ♔c5** (5 ♔c7 is also met by 5...♖a1) **5...♖a1** (not 5...♖a5+? 6 ♔b6 ♖a1 7 ♖c8, when White wins) **6 ♔b6** (6 g5 ♖a2 7 g6 ♖a1 doesn't change the situation) **6...♖b1+ 7 ♔c7 ♖c1+ 8 ♔d6 ♖d1+** Black is safe. Whenever the white king approaches the a-pawn, Black checks it away. This draw also operates if White has an h-pawn instead of a g-pawn.

43) 1 fxg3? ♖a2 is essentially the same draw as in the previous exercise, while 1 f4? is just a blunder since 1...♖xf4+ 2 ♔g2 ♖a4 draws. **1 f3!** is the only move to win. Then **1...♖a2** (trying to stop ♔g2 and ♔xg3) **2 f4** (Black has no way to prevent the advance of the f-pawn since his rook cannot leave the a-file without allowing ♖b8 followed by a8♕) **2...♔h7 3 f5 ♔g7 4 f6+!** (this is why an f-pawn wins whereas a g-pawn does not; Black cannot avoid the loss of his rook) **4...♔f7** (4...♔xf6 5 ♖f8+, or 4...♔h7 5 ♔g1 followed by f7) **5 ♖h8! ♖xa7 6 ♖h7+** and White wins the rook using the trick of Exercise 21.

44) **1 h7+?** was a bad mistake throwing away the win. Rook and two connected passed pawns normally win easily against a rook, but when the pawns are far-advanced you must take care not to deliver stalemate. After **1...♔h8** there's no good defence to the threat of 2...♖a6!; for example, **2 ♔h6 ♖a6 3 ♖f6 ♖xf6+ 4 gxf6** stalemate. White can only avoid this by giving up the h-pawn, when the position is a draw in any case (see Exercise 32). White could have won by playing **1 ♖b5 ♖a6+ 2 ♔h5 ♖a8 3 g6 ♖c8 4 ♔g5 ♖a8 5 h7+** (now is the right time for this) **5...♔g7** (or 5...♔h8 6 ♔h6) **6 ♖b7+ ♔h8 7 ♔h6** followed by mate.

45) The position is lost for Black. He is in zugzwang, since if he moves the rook, the pawn can advance, while if he moves his king then White's king can move forward. One possible line is **1...♔e7 2 ♔f5 ♔f7 3 ♖a1** (the key idea: White can play a waiting move with his rook, forcing Black to make a concession; 3 ♔e4 is less effective since 3...♔e6 keeps the white king out) **3...♔e7** (after 3...♔g7 4 ♔e4! Black cannot prevent White's king from reaching b5; for example, 4...♔g6 5 ♔d5 ♔g5 6 ♖a4! followed by ♔c5-b5 frees the a-pawn to advance) **4 ♔g6 ♔f8** (4...♔e6 5 ♖e1+ ♔d7 6 ♔f7 is similar to the main line) **5 ♖a2 ♔e7** (Black must let the king in to g7) **6 ♔g7 ♔e6 7 ♖e2+ ♔d7 8 ♔f7 ♖d6** (8...♖xa5 9 ♖d2+ ♔c7 10 ♔xf6 is similar) **9 ♖a2 ♖a6 10 ♖d2+ ♔c7 11 ♖f2 ♖xa5 12 ♔xf6 ♔d7 13 g5 ♔e8 14 ♔g6** and White will soon reach the Lucena position.

46) 1 ♔g2? ♖d2+! 2 ♔f3 ♖a2 3 ♖e8+ ♔g7 4 ♖a8 ♖a4 is a draw. Although White can now push his pawn to a7, the pawn then gets stuck since White cannot move his rook away from a8. 1 ♖e8+? ♔f7 2 ♖a8 (it's too late for 2 ♖e1 as 2...♖d3! threatens both ...♖xg3 and ...♖a3) 2...♖d3 3 ♔g2 ♖a3 amounts to the same thing. **1 ♖a3!** is correct. One guideline for rook endings that applies in almost every case is that if you have a passed pawn, you should put your rook behind it. Then the opponent must use one of his pieces to prevent the pawn's advance. After **1...♖a6** Black's rook cannot move without allowing the pawn to move forward, and **2 ♔g2 ♔f7 3 ♔f3 ♔e7 4 ♔f4 ♔e6 5 g4** reaches the position of the previous exercise.

47) Not 1 ♖d1? ♖c2+! 2 ♔g3 ♖a2 3 ♖d5 ♖a4 4 ♔f2 ♖a3 5 ♔e2 f5 and Black's rook ties the white pieces down by attacking a5 and f3, which prevents White from achieving anything. **1**

Ξ**d2!** is the only move which guarantees that White will be able to place his rook behind his own passed pawn, since this move cuts out Black's check on c2. After **1...⌖f5 2 Ξa2 Ξa6 3 ⌖g3** White wins by gradually forcing the enemy king back, much as in Exercise 46. One possible line is **3...⌖g5 4 f4+ ⌖f5 5 Ξa1 ⌖e6 6 ⌖g4 ⌖e7 7 ⌖f5 ⌖f7 8 Ξa2 ⌖e7 9 ⌖g6** and so on.

48) 1 Ξd7! is by far the best move and should be played before Black prevents it with 1...⌖e7. Piece activity is very important in rook endings, and there is nowhere better to put your rook than the seventh rank, where it can attack any enemy pawns still on their original squares. While it's too soon to say that White is winning, he certainly has a large advantage. Play might continue **1...Ξc8 2 c4** (2 ⌖e2? Ξe8+ 3 ⌖d3 Ξe7 lets Black escape) **2...h5 3 b4 g6** (trying to remove the pawns from the rook's attack) **4 c5 ⌖g8** (intending ...Ξf8+ and ...Ξf7) **5 ⌖e2 ⌖f8 6 ⌖f3**, followed by ⌖f4 and ⌖g5, and Black is in big trouble.

49) 1 ⌖g6? Ξxg4+ **2 ⌖xf6 ⌖g8** (this is like Exercise 38) **3 Ξa8+ ⌖h7 4 ⌖e6 Ξe4+ 5 ⌖f7 Ξb4** (Black uses the *principle of maximum checking distance*) **6 Ξa7 Ξb8 7 f6 ⌖h6** leads to a draw. Getting your king to an active position is often worth a pawn and here **1 g5! fxg5 2 ⌖g6** wins since now there is no check on g4, so White can force through f6, threatening mate on the back rank. After **2...g4** (there's nothing better) **3 f6 Ξb8 4 Ξh7 ⌖g8 5 f7+ ⌖f8 6 Ξh8+** White wins the rook.

50) White would like to attack the black pawns with his king, but they form a solid wall keeping the white king out. By pushing the h-pawn, White can blow a hole in the wall and gain entry for his king: **1 h5! gxh5+** (1...f5+ 2 exf5 gxh5+ 3 ⌖xh5 Ξf6 4 ⌖g4 followed by ⌖f4 and ⌖e5 also wins for White) **2 ⌖f5!** (this is simplest, although 2 ⌖xh5 should also win) **2...⌖b7** (Black dare not give up the f-pawn as White would then have two connected passed pawns) **3 f4 Ξc6 4 Ξh1** (Black's pawns are all weak and fall one by one) **4...⌖c7 5 Ξxh5 ⌖d7 6 Ξxh6 ⌖e7 7 e5** followed by Ξxf6, with an easy win for White.

51) In rook endings, connected passed pawns are generally far more powerful than disconnected ones. 1 exd5? only draws even though it wins a pawn. Black replies 1...⌖b5 2 d6 ⌖c6 3 Ξd1 ⌖d7 4 Ξd5 Ξf6 5 ⌖b4 Ξxd6 and his problems are over. Instead, **1 e5!** is correct. After **1...⌖b5 2 f6 ⌖c6 3 e6 ⌖d6 4 Ξe1** (this is simplest, although 4 e7 also wins) **4...Ξa8+** (or 4...Ξxf6 5 e7) **5 ⌖b4 Ξb8+ 6 ⌖c3 Ξc8+ 7 ⌖d2** there's nothing Black can do to prevent e7 followed by f7, when one of the pawns promotes.

52) Zugzwang occurs most often in pawn endings, but it is also common in rook endings. Here White wins not by taking the pawn on g6, but by putting Black in zugzwang and so winning both Black's kingside pawns: **1 ⌖f4!** (1 ⌖xg6? f4 is an easy draw) **1...g5+** (Black's pawns must commit suicide, since 1...⌖h4 allows 2 Ξh2# while 1...Ξb8 2 b7 only repeats the zugzwang) **2 ⌖xg5** (2 ⌖xf5? g4 lets one pawn get away) **2...⌖g3 3 ⌖xf5** followed by playing the king to c6, freeing White's pawn to advance.

53) With four rooks on the board, there are tactical ideas that are simply not possible with only two rooks. Here White's b-pawn appears doomed but **1 Ξf1!** turns the tables. The pinned rook is now doubly attacked and has nowhere to go, so White wins a rook.

54) If one rook on the seventh rank is dangerous, two are terrifying. Here the attacking power of the rooks outweighs the imminent promotion of Black's pawn: **1 Ξg7+ ⌖f8** (or 1...⌖h8 2 Ξh7+ ⌖g8 3 Ξcg7+ ⌖f8 4 h6 followed by Ξh8#) **2 Ξh7!** (Black has no time to promote as he must deal with the threat of Rh8#) **2...♔g8 3 Rcg7+** (3 h6 first is equally good) **3...♔f8 4 h6** and now that the rook on g7 is defended, there's no way Black can prevent Rh8#.

55) It's not easy to decide the right square for White's king. 1 ♔b4? doesn't offer enough support for White's own pawn, and Black wins by 1...♔d3 2 a5 ♔d4 3 ♔b5 ♔d5 4 ♔b6 ♔d6 5 a6 Rb1+ 6 ♔a7 ♔c7 7 ♔a8 Rb8+ 8 ♔a7 Rb6 9 ♔a8 Rxa6#. 1 ♔b6? appears most natural but allows Black's king to approach too quickly: 1...♔d3 2 a5 ♔c4 3 a6 Rh6+ 4 ♔b7 ♔b5 5 a7 Rh7+ 6 ♔b8 ♔b6 with the win of Exercise 3. The 'Goldilocks' move **1 ♔b5!** is correct. After **1...Rb1+ 2 ♔c5 Ra1** (Black transfers his rook to a1 with gain of time) **3 ♔b5 ♔d3 4 a5 ♔d4 5 a6 ♔d5 6 ♔b6 ♔d6 7 ♔b7!** (7 a7? Rb1+ 8 ♔a6 ♔c7! wins for Black after 9 a8♕ Ra1+ or 9 a8♘+ ♔c6 10 ♔a7 Rb2 and the knight is lost) **7...Rb1+ 8 ♔c8!** (the only move to draw) **8...Ra1 9 ♔b7 ♔d7 10 a7 Rb1+ 11 ♔a8!** White scrapes a draw.

56) The astonishing drawing line is **1...♔d3!!** (Black blocks his own pawn, but it's more important to shoulder White's king away than to push the pawn; 1...d3? loses to 2 ♔f5 ♔c3 3 ♔e4 d2 4 ♔e3) **2 ♔f5 ♔e3 3 ♔g4** (3 Rh8 d3 4 Rh3+ ♔e2 5 ♔e4 d2 6 Rh2+ ♔e1 7 ♔e3 d1♘+ is a draw as in Exercise 2) **3...d3 4 ♔g3 d2 5 ♔g2 ♔e2** and Black saves the game.

57) The natural instinct is to move your king towards the enemy pawn, but here 1...♔e7? loses to 2 a6 Ra5 3 a7, when the black king is caught in the open with no defence to the coming 4 Rh8 Rxa7 5 Rh7+ skewer (3...♔f6 loses at once to 4 Rf8+). **1...♔g7!** is the only drawing move. If the white king approaches the a-pawn to free the rook, then Black just delivers checks with his rook from the f-file, while after **2 a6 Rf6!** we have the draw of Exercise 41.

58) 1 Ra5 is met by 1...♔e8, preventing ♔f7, and now White should continue 2 Ra8+ ♔d7 3 Rf8, returning to the correct plan. 1 ♔g6? is even worse, as it throws the win away after 1...♔e7! 2 Ra7+ ♔f8 3 ♔f6 ♔g8 4 Ra8+ ♔h7. The best line is **1 Rf8!** (this odd move is the only way to reach the Lucena position) **1...Rf2** (Black can only wait; 1...Rg1 2 ♔f7 followed by f6 is no better) **2 ♔g7 Rg2+** (the point of 1 Rf8 is that White can meet 2...♔e7 with 3 f6+) **3 ♔f7 Rf2 4 f6 Rg2 5 Rg8 Ra2 6 ♔g7 Rg2+ 7 ♔f8** and White will reach the Lucena position.

59) 1 f4? a3 followed by ...Ra4 allows Black to get his rook behind the pawn, after which Black wins. Also not 1 Rh1? ♔g7! 2 Rb1 (this is too slow, since Rb6 is not a threat when the g6-pawn is defended) 2...Rc7!, followed by ...Ra7, and Black wins much as in Exercise 46 (with colours reversed). When you have a passed pawn, you should put your own rook behind it. The same principle applies when fighting against an enemy passed pawn: you should put your own rook behind the enemy pawn. Here **1 Rb1!** achieves this, because there are two threats: 2 Rb8+ followed by Ra8, and 2 Rb6, attacking the g6-pawn, followed by Ra6, and Black cannot prevent both (1 Rd1! draws the same way and is just as good). Then both **1...Rc6 2 Rb8+ ♔e7 3 Ra8 Rc4 4 Ra6** and **1...♔e7 2 Rb6 g5 3 Ra6** lead to a draw.

60) White can win. The attacking power of the rooks is so great that he can win a rook by force: **1 Rg7+ ♔h8** (1...♔f8 loses to 2 Rdf7+ ♔e8 3 Rf3! and there is no real answer to the threat of Rg8+; for example, 3...Rd8 4 Rg8+ ♔e7 5 Re3+ ♔d7 6 Rd3+ and White wins a rook in any case) **2 Rh7+ ♔g8 3 Rdg7+ ♔f8 4 Rg4!** (threatening 5 Rh8+; White must secure the maximum checking distance, since 4 Rg5? fails after 4...Re8 5 Rh8+ ♔f7 6 Rf5+ ♔g6 and the f5-rook is attacked) **4...Re8** (4...Rd8 5 Rh8+ ♔e7 6 Re4+ is also winning for White) **5 Rh8+ ♔f7 6 Rf4+ ♔e7 7 Re4+** and White wins.

5 Rook and Minor Piece Endings

There are many possible combinations of rooks and minor pieces. In this chapter we focus mainly on four of the most important, ♖ vs ♗, ♖ vs ♘, ♖+♗ vs ♖ and ♖+♘ vs ♖. If there are no pawns on the board then all four of these endings are usually drawn, but in the case of ♖ vs ♘ and ♖+♗ vs ♖ there are also many winning positions.

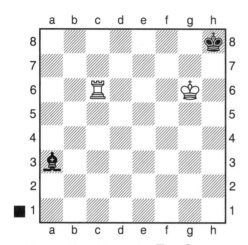 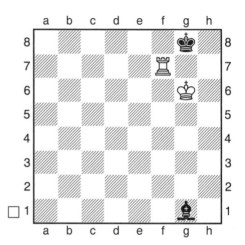

Almost all positions with ♖ vs ♗ (without pawns) are drawn, but the rook sometimes wins if the defender's king is stuck in the corner. Then the result depends on which corner the king occupies. If the bishop moves on the same coloured squares as the corner square (this is the case in this diagram), then the rook wins. Here there's no real defence to the threat of ♖c8+ followed by mate. If **1...♗f8**, then **2 ♖c8 ♔g8 3 ♖b8** (or any square on the eighth rank) places Black in zugzwang. He must play **3...♔h8**, allowing **4 ♖xf8#**.

However, if you move the bishop to a2 in the diagram (so that it moves on squares of opposite colour to the corner square) then the position is a draw. Black just waits by **1...♗b3**. After **2 ♖c8+ ♗g8** White must lift the stalemate, but this frees either the king or the bishop. However White plays, he can never do better than to stalemate Black.

This formation is important because you can move the bishop to any dark square and have either player to move, but White wins every time. The diagram position is one of the more difficult cases. White wins by **1 ♖f1 ♗h2** (if the bishop comes out into the open, White wins by skewering the bishop against the threat of mate on the eighth rank; for example, 1...♗d4 2 ♖d1 ♗b6 3 ♖b1 ♗c7 4 ♖c1 and the bishop is lost; it follows that Black must try to keep the bishop on the f-, g- or h-file) **2 ♖h1 ♗g3 3 ♖h3 ♗f2** (now that the bishop has been chased to the f-file, White can change tack) **4 ♖a3 ♔f8** (or 4...♗c5 5 ♖a8+ ♗f8 6 ♖b8) **5 ♖f3+** and the bishop is lost. This final fork explains why White had to chase the bishop to the f-file before threatening mate on the back rank.

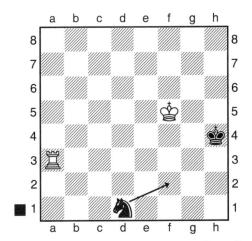

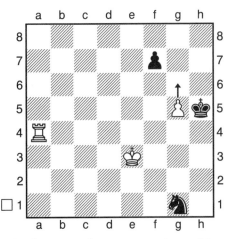

Likewise, most positions with ♖ vs ♘ are drawn, but here there are more winning chances. Indeed, if the knight is far away from its own king then most positions are lost. When playing with the knight, the crucial point is to keep the knight near your king. Then you will draw, except if your king is badly placed on the edge of the board or, even worse, stuck in a corner. The diagram shows a marginal case. Black can draw, but only if he moves his knight towards his king. 1...♘b2? is too far away; then 2 ♖a2 ♘d1 (after 2...♘c4 3 ♖a4 White picks up the knight at once, while 2...♘d3 3 ♖a4+ ♔h5 4 ♖a3 ♘f2 5 ♖f3 wins the knight or mates) 3 ♖d2 ♘e3+ (3...♘c3 loses to 4 ♖d4+ ♔h5 5 ♖d3) 4 ♔f4 ♘g4 (4...♘f1 5 ♖f2) 5 ♖g2 wins the knight, since if it moves White mates by ♖h2#. The correct drawing line is 1...♘f2! 2 ♖f3 ♘h3! (the only move to draw) 3 ♖e3 ♘f2 4 ♔f4 ♘h3+ and White cannot win. Whenever White's pieces start to occupy dangerous positions, Black always has a knight check to drive the white king away.

Tactics are rather common in positions with rooks and minor pieces and you must be alert to spot any opportunities that arise. Here White is material up, but if he loses his pawn for nothing then the result will be a draw. Simply defending the pawn by 1 ♖a5? doesn't work because after 1...♘h3 there is no way to save the pawn. Nor does chasing the knight by 1 ♔f2? ♘h3+ 2 ♔g3 ♘xg5 achieve anything. Often the right move can be found by taking an idea that doesn't work and modifying it into one that does, for example by playing a preliminary move. Here the winning idea is **1 g6!**. Then 1...♔xg6 loses the knight to 2 ♖g4+, so **1...fxg6** is forced. Now the knight-chasing idea is lethal because after **2 ♔f2! ♘h3+ 3 ♔g3 ♘g5** (3...♘g1 4 ♖a2 followed by ♖g2 picks up the knight) the g6-square is blocked by Black's pawn and White can mate by **4 ♖h4#**.

Exercises

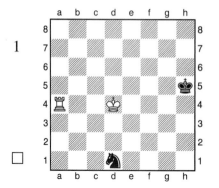

1

How does White trap and win the black knight?

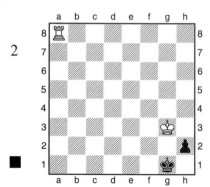

2

Can Black save the day by 1...h1♞+?

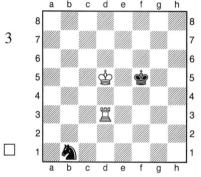

3

Which is best, 1 ♔c4 or 1 ♔c5?

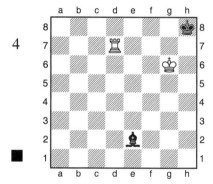

4

Can Black draw this position?

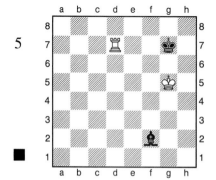

5

Black is in check. Which king move should he play?

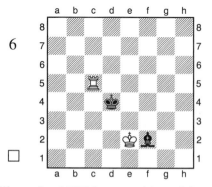

6

Where should White move his rook?

74

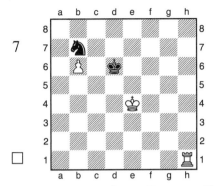

7

Is the correct move 1 ♔d4, 1 ♖h6+ or 1 ♖c1?

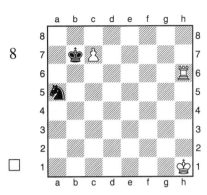

8

Find the winning move for White.

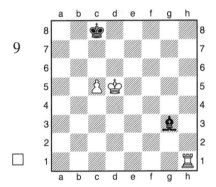

9

Which is better, 1 c6 or 1 ♔c6?

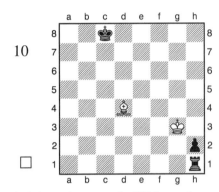

10

Find the only move for White to draw.

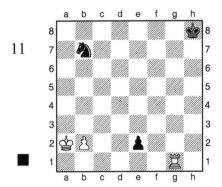

11

If White can take the e-pawn for nothing then he will win. How can Black prevent this?

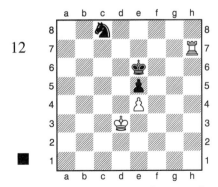

12

Should Black continue 1...♘e7, 1...♘d6 or 1...♔d6?

75

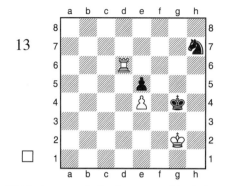

13

White's pawn is in danger as Black intends ...♚f4. How can White win?

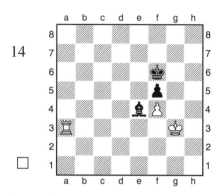

14

Can White win this position?

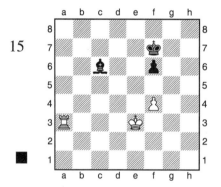

15

On general principles, which move is best for Black: 1...f5, 1...♚g6 or 1...♝d7?

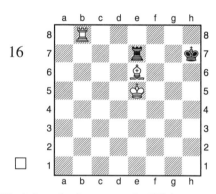

16

Find the winning move for White.

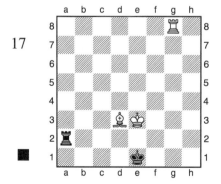

17

Find the only saving move for Black.

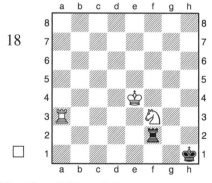

18

How does White win?

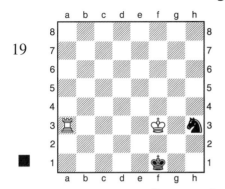

19

Which move is correct: 1...♘g1+, 1...♘g5+ or 1...♔e1?

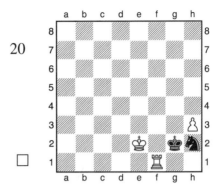

20

Find the only move that wins for White.

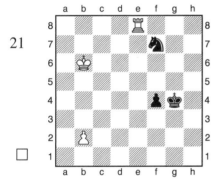

21

On general principles, is the best move 1 b4, 1 ♔c5 or 1 ♖f8?

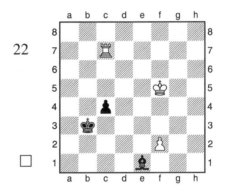

22

Should White play 1 f3 or 1 f4?

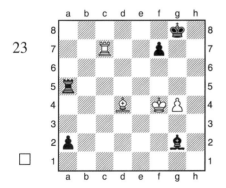

23

White looks to be in trouble, but he has a forced win. What should he play?

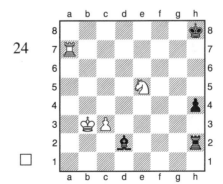

24

Find the winning move for White.

Solutions to Rook and Minor Piece Ending Exercises

1) **1 ♖a2!** covers b2 and f2 and so totally immobilizes the black knight. After **1...♔g4** (Black tries to rescue the knight using his king, but his majesty arrives too late) **2 ♖d2!** the knight will be captured next move. When playing with king and knight against king and rook, you must keep the knight near your king. Once the king and knight are separated, the knight can easily be trapped and lost.

2) Black is losing. With his king and knight both stuck in the corner there is no way to save the game: **1...h1♘+ 2 ♔f3 ♔h2** (or 2...♘f2 3 ♖a1+) **3 ♖g8** and White wins the knight, since **3...♔h3** allows **4 ♖h8#**.

3) White should play **1 ♔c5!** (1 ♔c4? ♔e4 is only a draw as White must now move his rook, allowing the knight to escape; for example, 2 ♖d8 ♘a3+ 3 ♔b3 ♘b5) **1...♔e4** (1...♔f4 loses to 2 ♔d4 ♔f5 3 ♔e3 followed by ♖b3) **2 ♔c4!** (now Black is in zugzwang) **2...♔f4 3 ♔b3** followed by ♖d1 and the knight is lost.

4) Black can draw by **1...♗c4!**. ♖ vs ♗ looks dangerous when the defender's king is trapped in the corner, but as mentioned on page 72 he is generally safe so long as the bishop is on an opposite-coloured square to the corner square. After **2 ♖d8+ ♗g8 3 ♖d7** (White must lift the stalemate) **3...♗b3** (but not 3...♗e6? 4 ♖h7+ ♔g8 5 ♖e7 and White wins because Black has no check on the b1-h7 diagonal) **4 ♖h7+ ♔g8 5 ♖b7 ♗c2+** the white king must move, destroying the mating threat. So long as Black takes a little care, he should have little trouble reaching a draw.

5) The situation is quite different when the bishop moves on the same coloured squares as the corner square. If the defender's king gets stuck in such a corner, he almost always loses. Here 1...♔h8? loses to 2 ♔g6 ♗b6 3 ♖e7 followed by ♖e8+. 1...♔g8? 2 ♔g6 is little better; for example, 2...♔f8 3 ♖f7+, 2...♗b6 3 ♖b7 ♗d8 4 ♖b8, 2...♗c5 3 ♖d8+ ♗f8 4 ♖a8 and mate next move or 2...♗h4 3 ♖d4! ♗e7 (the only way to maintain control of d8) 4 ♖a4 ♔f8 5 ♖a8+ and White wins in every line. The king must escape from the dangerous h8-corner as quickly as possible, so Black should play **1...♔f8!**. Then **2 ♔f6 ♗h4+ 3 ♔e6 ♗g5** is a draw as White cannot drive Black's king back towards h8.

6) **1 ♖g5!** is the only square to trap the bishop. After **1...♗e3 2 ♖g4+** or **1...♗h4 2 ♖g4+** the bishop is lost.

7) It's not always easy to win with ♖+♙ vs ♘ if your king cannot support the pawn. Here 1 ♔d4? ♔c6! 2 ♖h6+ (or 2 ♖b1 ♘a5) 2...♔b5 is a draw as the white king cannot reach c7 without crossing the sixth rank, at which point Black can just take the pawn. 1 ♖h6+? ♔c5 2 ♔e5 ♘a5 is much the same. The winning line is **1 ♖c1!** (White uses the power of the rook to cut off the enemy king, much as in Chapter 4) **1...♘a5 2 ♖c2** (waiting for the knight to return to b7) **2...♘b7 3 ♖c7 ♘a5 4 ♔d4** (now the king can move to support the pawn while keeping the enemy king cut off) **4...♘c6+ 5 ♔c4 ♘d8 6 ♔b5** and White wins.

8) Simply defending the pawn by 1 ♖h7? isn't good enough as Black can round up the c-pawn with 1...♘c4 2 ♔g2 ♘b6 3 ♔f3 ♘d5 followed by ...♘xc7, with a draw. However, after **1 ♖a6!** there's no good square for the knight, and the lines **1...♘c6 2 ♖xc6, 1...♘c4 2 c8♕+** (2 ♖c6 also wins) **2...♔xc8 3 ♖c6+** and **1...♘b3 2 ♖b6+!** all win for White.

9) 1 c6? unexpectedly allows Black to draw by simply keeping his bishop on the h2-b8 diagonal. It turns out that White cannot achieve anything as the pawn prevents the king from moving to c6, while if the king gets to b6, Black just checks it away again. After 1...♗f4 the best winning try is 2 ♔c5 ♗e5 3 ♔b6 ♗d4+ 4 ♔b5 ♗e5 5 ♖h7 ♗f4 6 c7, since now 6...♗xc7? loses to 7 ♔c6 ♗a5 8 ♖h8+ ♗d8 9 ♖g8. However, Black draws by playing 6...♔b7! and only then ...♗xc7, since he avoids having his king trapped on the back rank. **1 ♔c6!** is better and leads to a quick win. In positions such as this, you should have your king in front of the pawn, as in pure pawn endings (see Exercise 8 on page 17, for example). After **1...♔d8 2 ♔b7 ♗f4 3 ♖h7**, followed by c6 and c7, White wins the bishop.

10) Black is threatening to play 1...♖d1, intending either ...♖xd4 or ...h1♕, and so winning the bishop. If the bishop stands on any square where it can be attacked by the rook, the same idea works; for example, 1 ♗f2? ♖f1! or 1 ♗g7? ♖g1+. Amazingly, hiding in the corner by **1 ♗h8!** is the one way to save the game. Only on h8 is the bishop safe from attack. Now White can continue with 2 ♔g2 and win the h-pawn, after which he has a standard ♖ vs ♗ draw.

11) The only move to draw uses the forking power of the knight: **1...♘c5!** (threatening 2...♘d3 followed by ...e1♕) **2 ♖e1 ♘d3 3 ♖xe2 ♘c1+** and Black wins the rook and draws. Knights are tricky beasts and you must watch out for possible forks.

12) In order to draw a position like this, the knight must be placed where it both attacks the white pawn, tying one of White's pieces down to its defence, and keeps the enemy king out. It follows that d6 is the ideal square for the knight, and Black should not delay in occupying it. 1...♘e7? is too slow and loses after 2 ♖h8 (preventing both ...♘c8-d6 and ...♘g8-f6) 2...♘g6 3 ♖h6 ♔f7 4 ♔c4 ♘f4 (trying to keep control of d5) 5 ♔c5 ♔e7 6 ♔c6 ♘g2 7 ♖h8 (7 ♔d5? ♘e3+! draws since 8 ♔xe5 ♘g4+ costs White the rook) 7...♘f4 8 ♖a8 ♘d3 9 ♔d5 and White will soon win the e-pawn. 1...♔d6? is also bad since 2 ♖h6+ ♔d7 3 ♔c4 ♘e7 4 ♔c5 ♔c7 5 ♖e6 again picks up the e-pawn. The way to draw is **1...♘d6! 2 ♖h6+ ♔e7 3 ♖h5 ♔e6**, when White cannot make progress as his king must always defend e4.

13) White wins by **1 ♔f2!** (threatening 2 ♔e3, which would secure White's pawn and leave him in a winning position) **1...♘f4** (1...♘g5 2 ♔e3 is hopeless for Black as his king is badly placed; for example, 2...♘f7 3 ♖d7 ♘h6 4 ♖e7 and the pawn falls) **2 ♖h6! ♘g5** (2...♘f8 loses the knight after 3 ♖f6+) **3 ♖h4#** with a surprise mate.

14) White can win. It's a big advantage for White to have Black's pawn stuck on a light square, the same colour as the squares the bishop moves on, since then the dark squares can only be defended by the black king. White can use rook checks to drive the opposing king back, allowing his own king to advance. Here's a typical line: **1 ♖a6+ ♔f7 2 ♔h4 ♗d3 3 ♖b6 ♗e4 4 ♔g5 ♗d3 5 ♖c6** (White wants to take on f5 to reach a won pawn ending, but 5 ♖f6+ ♔g7 6 ♖xf5? is too soon since 6...♗xf5 7 ♔xf5 ♔f7 is only a draw – see Exercise 7 on page 17) **5...♗b1** (Black can only wait) **6 ♖c5 ♔g7** (6...♗e4 7 ♖xf5+ ♗xf5 8 ♔xf5 is a win for White as he has the opposition) **7 ♖c7+ ♔f8 8 ♔f6 ♔e8 9 ♖e7+ ♔d8** (after 9...♔f8 10 ♖b7 White wins the bishop) **10 ♖e5 ♔d7 11 ♖xf5 ♗xf5 12 ♔xf5** and White wins.

15) 1...f5? is clearly wrong, since then White can win as in the previous exercise. Black needs to keep his pawn on a dark square, so that it can work together with the bishop, which operates on light squares. Between them, the bishop and pawn can make a barrier that prevents the white king from advancing to a dangerous position. Black would ideally like his bishop on the longer b1-h7 diagonal, but there is a trap. 1...♗d7? is certainly the right idea, aiming for f5, but it allows 2 ♖a7! ♔e8 (2...♔e6 3 f5+ ♔d6 4 ♔f4 ♗e8 5 ♖h7! puts Black in zugzwang, as moving the bishop along the a4-e8 diagonal allows ♖f7, while any king move allows ♖h6) 3 ♔e4 and Black is in trouble since his king is now cut off on the back rank. White can win, although it still requires some work; one line is 3...♗e6 4 ♖a3 ♗g4 5 f5 ♔e7 6 ♖a7+ ♔f8 7 ♖h7 ♔e8 8 ♖h4 ♗d1 9 ♔d5 ♗b3+ 10 ♔d6 ♗a2 11 ♖b4 ♔f8 12 ♔c5 ♔e7 13 ♖b7+ ♔f8 14 ♖b2 (it turns out that the bishop doesn't have a safe square on the a2-g8 diagonal) 14...♗f7 15 ♖b8+ ♔e7 16 ♖b7+ ♔f8 17 ♖xf7+ ♔xf7 18 ♔d6 with a winning pawn ending (see Exercise 18 on page 18). **1...♔g6!** is the only move to draw, since there is no way to prevent the bishop from safely reaching f5. After **2 ♖a5 ♗d7 3 ♔d4 ♗f5** Black has no problems; for example, **4 ♔d5 ♔h5** followed by ...♔g4 draws.

16) Although ♖+♗ vs ♖ is usually a draw, there are many winning positions when the defending king is on the edge of the board or in a corner. Here **1 ♔f6!** is the decisive move. White both attacks the rook and threatens to launch a mating attack starting with ♗f5+. There's no defence; for example, **1...♖a7 2 ♗f5+ ♔h6 3 ♖h8+ ♖h7 4 ♖xh7#**.

17) Black is on the brink of defeat due to his badly placed king, but **1...♖e2+!** saves the day. Using a stalemate trick, Black forces the white king away and gains a respite. After **2 ♔f3** (or 2 ♔d4 ♖h2) **2...♖f2+ 3 ♔e4 ♖h2** the black king slips away from the back rank to d2 or f2. If you are defending this ending and your king gets stuck on the edge of the board, then a good defensive plan is to put your rook on the rank (or file, if your king is on the a- or h-file) just in front of your king.

18) Just like ♖+♗ vs ♖, the ending of ♖+♘ vs ♖ is generally drawn, but there are a few winning positions, especially with the defending king in a corner. Here White can win with a direct attack on the king: **1 ♖a1+ ♔g2 2 ♖g1+ ♔h3 3 ♔f4** (threatening 4 ♖g3#) **3...♖g2 4 ♖h1+ ♖h2 5 ♖xh2#**.

19) The ending ♖ vs ♘ is generally drawn if the king and knight are close to each other. This position is rather unfavourable for Black as his king is badly placed on the edge of the board, so he must take care that his king and knight do not get separated. 1...♘g5+? 2 ♔f4 ♘e6+ 3 ♔e5 leaves the king and knight far apart and allows White to win by 3...♘c5 4 ♔d5 ♘d7 5 ♖a6 ♔e2 6 ♖d6 ♘f8 7 ♔e5 ♘h7 8 ♔f5 ♔e3 9 ♖d7 ♘f8 10 ♖f7 and the knight falls. 1...♔e1? is also bad since 2 ♔g3 ♘g5 (2...♘f2 3 ♖e3+ ♔f1 4 ♖f3) 3 ♔g4 ♘f7 (3...♘e4 4 ♖e3+) 4 ♖e3+ ♔d2 5 ♖e7 ♘h6+ (or 5...♘d6 6 ♖d7) 6 ♔g5 ♘g8 7 ♖g7 wins the same way. **1...♘g1+!** is the only move to draw; after **2 ♔e3** (2 ♔g3 ♘e2+ 3 ♔g4 ♔f2 is also a draw) **2...♔g2** Black escapes from the edge of the board and is now safe.

20) Most moves of the attacked rook are met by ...♔xh3, when it's a draw even though the black king is on the edge of the board; for example, 1 ♖f8? ♔xh3 2 ♖g8 ♘g4 3 ♔f3 ♘h2+ 4 ♔f4 ♘f1! draws as in the previous exercise. However, the astonishing **1 ♖h1!** wins the game, since **1...♔xh1** (1...♔xh3 2 ♔f2 wins the knight, while 1...♘f3 2 h4! ♘d4+ 3 ♔e3 ♘f5+ 4 ♔f4 also wins as the h-pawn is free to advance) **2 ♔f2** puts Black in zugzwang. All three legal moves lose the knight, after which White promotes the h-pawn.

21) When both sides have passed pawns, it's often necessary to use your king to fight against the enemy pawn. Here Black's pawn is further advanced than White's, so in a straight race Black will promote first. By using his king and rook, White can hold Black up long enough to give his own pawn a head start. **1 ♔c5!** (1 b4? f3 2 ♖f8 ♘e5 3 ♔c7 ♔g3 4 b5 ♘c4 5 b6 ♘xb6 6 ♔xb6 f2 7 ♔c5 ♔g2 is an easy draw for Black, and 1 ♖f8? ♘e5 2 ♔c7 f3 3 b4 ♘d3 4 b5 f2, threatening 5...♘f4, leads to a draw after 5 ♖xf2 ♘xf2 6 b6 ♘d3 7 b7 ♘c5 8 b8♕ ♘a6+) **1...f3 2 ♖f8 ♘g5** (2...♘e5 3 ♔d4 ♘d7 4 ♖f7 is also winning) **3 ♔c4!** (not 3 ♔d4?? ♘e6+) **3...♔g3 4 ♔d3** (now the white king is nearby, and Black finds it hard to do anything with his f-pawn) **4...f2 5 ♔e2 ♘h3 6 ♔f1** and the king's march from b5 to f1 has brought Black's pawn to a dead stop. White now has an easy win; for example, **6...♘f4 7 b4 ♘d5 8 b5 ♘e3+ 9 ♔e2 ♘d5 10 ♖f3+ ♔g4 11 ♔xf2** and so on.

22) As in Exercise 21, White cannot win an immediate pawn race as Black is currently ahead, so White must use his king to hold up the c-pawn. If White could get his king to d3 without losing the f-pawn then he would win, and to achieve this the white pawn needs to be on a square where it cannot be attacked by the enemy bishop. White wins by **1 f3!** (after 1 f4? c3 2 ♔e4 ♗d2! White must waste a move playing f5 before he can move his king to d3, and 3 f5 c2 4 f6 c1♕ 5 ♖xc1 ♗xc1 6 f7 ♗a3 gives Black just enough time to draw) **1...c3 2 ♔e4! ♗d2 3 ♔d3** (Black's c-pawn cannot advance further) **3...♔b2 4 ♖c8** (a waiting move) **4...♔b3 5 ♖c4 ♔b2 6 f4 ♔b3 7 f5** and now the advance of the f-pawn is decisive.

23) When there are additional rooks or queens on the board, opposite-coloured bishops can lend force to an attack. Here White strikes before Black can make use of his far-advanced a-pawn: **1 ♖c8+ ♔h7 2 ♖h8+ ♔g6 3 ♖g8+ ♔h7** (or 3...♔h6 4 g5+ and Black must give up his rook since 4...♔h5 5 ♖h8+ ♔g6 6 ♖h6# and 4...♔h7 5 ♖h8+ ♔g6 6 ♖h6# both lead to mate) **4 ♖g7+ ♔h6** (4...♔h8 5 ♖g5+ costs Black his rook) **5 g5+ ♔h5** (5...♖xg5 6 ♖xg5 is also hopeless for Black) **6 ♖h7+ ♔g6 7 ♖h6#.**

24) The more material there is on the board, the greater the possibility of a direct attack on the enemy king. A typical ♖+♘ mating pattern against a king on h8 involves a rook on the seventh rank and the knight on f6, supporting mate by ♖h7#. In this position White can transfer his knight from e5 to f6 with gain of time, since **1 ♘g4!** attacks the enemy rook: **1...♖h3** (there is nothing better as 1...♗e3 loses to 2 ♖a8+ ♔g7 3 ♘xh2) **2 ♘f6 ♖xc3+ 3 ♔b2** with mate in a few moves.

SHOULDERING AWAY

81

6 Queen Endings

Queen endings can result when all the other pieces have been swapped off, or from a simpler ending when both sides promote. In this chapter we consider both pure queen endings and those involving the queen in combination with other pieces.

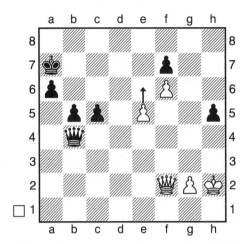

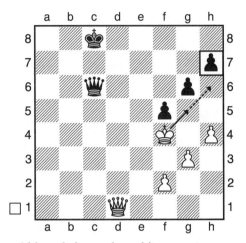

Passed pawns are extremely powerful in queen endings because the queen has the ability to force a passed pawn home without support from other pieces (see, for example, Exercise 14). This applies especially if the enemy king is too far away to lend a hand in fighting against the pawn. Here White is two pawns down but has a winning position because after **1 e6!** he creates a passed pawn that is further advanced than any black pawn. After **1...♛c4** (1...fxe6 2 f7 and 1...♛e4 2 exf7 ♛e5+ 3 ♛g3 ♛xf6 4 ♛c7+ ♚a8 5 ♛c8+ ♚a7 6 f8♛ also win for White) **2 e7 ♛e6 3 ♛xc5+ ♚b8** (or 3...♚b7 4 e8♛! ♛xe8 5 ♛e7+ ♛xe7 6 fxe7 and White will make another queen) there are several ways to win. Perhaps the neatest is **4 ♛b6+! ♛xb6 5 e8♛+ ♚c7 6 ♛xf7+ ♚c8** (after 6...♚c6 7 ♛e6+ White swaps queens and wins) **7 ♛e8+ ♚c7 8 ♛e7+ ♚c8 9 f7 ♛b8+ 10 g3** and the f-pawn promotes, with a win for White.

Although it can be a bit scary to move your king up the board when your opponent has a queen, king activity is at least as important in queen endings as in any other ending. Here White wins by marching his king to h6 and laying siege to Black's pawn on h7. Note that Black's king is cut off by the white queen much as in a rook ending. **1 ♚g5! ♛c5 2 ♚h6** (simply ignoring the attack on f2) **2...♛xf2** (2...♛f8+ 3 ♚xh7 ♛f7+ 4 ♚h6 is hopeless for Black since if he keeps checking then White just takes all the pawns with his king) **3 ♛b3!** (a dual-purpose move, defending g3 and intending ♛g8+ followed by ♛xh7+) **3...♛c5 4 ♛g8+ ♚c7 5 ♛xh7+ ♚d8 6 ♛xg6** and White's passed h-pawn, supported by king and queen, is decisive. The continuation might be **6...♚e7 7 ♚h7 ♛f2 8 h5 ♛f3 9 h6 ♛d5 10 ♛g7+ ♚d6 11 ♛f6+ ♚d7 12 ♚g6** followed by h7 with an easy win.

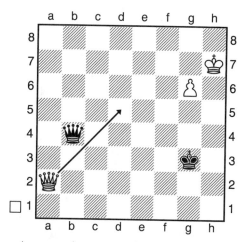

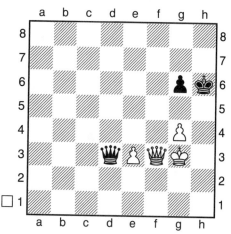

A queen is most actively placed in the middle of the board. White cannot win with 1 g7? since 1...♕e4+ 2 ♔h8 ♕h4+ 3 ♔g8 ♕d8+ 4 ♔f7 ♕d7+ 5 ♔f6 ♕d4+ 6 ♔g6 ♕e4+ is perpetual check. When the white queen is so far offside, there are no real chances to meet a black check with a queen interposition. The only winning move is 1 ♕d5!, occupying the centre. After 1...♕b1 (pinning the pawn is the best chance, since after 1...♕h4+ 2 ♔g8 there are no checks and the pawn can safely advance) 2 ♔h6 ♕b6 (continuing the pinning strategy) 3 ♕e5+ (3 ♔h5 ♕b2 is not clear, so White improves his queen position before playing ♔h5) 3...♔g4 4 ♕g5+ (from a central square, the queen can pick and choose the best check) 4...♔f3 5 ♔h5 (now Black cannot pin the pawn) 5...♕b7 6 g7 the win is relatively easy. One possible line runs 6...♕f7+ 7 ♔g6 ♕d5+ 8 ♔h6 ♕d2+ 9 ♕g5 ♕d6+ 10 ♔h5 ♕h2+ 11 ♔g6 ♕a2 (Black loses straight away after 11...♕d6+ 12 ♕f6+ or 11...♕c2+ 12 ♕f5+) 12 ♕f5+ ♔e3 13 ♔f6 (threatening ♕e6+) 13...♔d4 14 ♕g4+ followed by g8♕ and White wins.

One important word of caution applies especially to queen endings. Mate rarely occurs in endings and it's easy to forget that you still must take care of your king even when there are few pieces on the board. Queens are powerful pieces and can conjure up a mate even with limited assistance from king and pawns. The above position, taken from a recent tournament game, is a good example. Black is a pawn down but there are few pawns left and Black's pieces are in active positions, so the result should be a draw. White continued 1 ♕f4+ ♔h7 (1...♔g7? 2 ♕d4+ gives White a winning king and pawn ending) 2 ♕f7+ and now the correct move is 2...♔h8, when Black is in no danger at all. Instead Black moved his king the wrong way by 2...♔h6? and was taken aback when White forced mate in four moves: 3 g5+! ♔h5 (3...♔xg5 4 ♕f4+ is one move shorter) 4 ♕f3+! ♔xg5 5 ♕f4+ ♔h5 6 ♕h4#. Countless games have been lost to this type of 'endgame blindness' in which a player loses sight of the fact that it's possible to mate even in the endgame.

Exercises

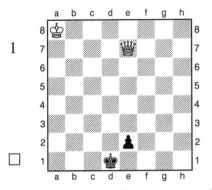

1

Black's pawn is threatening to promote. Can White win?

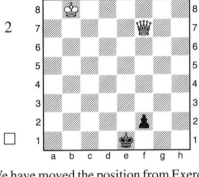

2

We have moved the position from Exercise 1 one file to the right. Is it still a win?

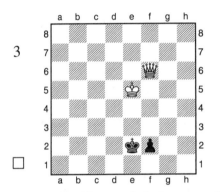

3

With the white king much further away this would be a draw, but can White win in this position?

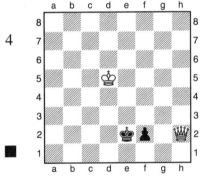

4

Which move is best: 1...♔e1, 1...♔f3 or 1...♔e3?

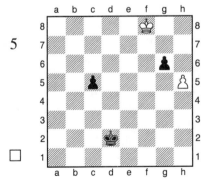

5

Which move is correct: 1 hxg6 or 1 h6?

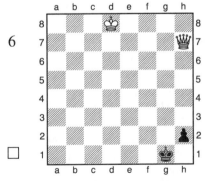

6

Can White win with a queen against a rook's pawn on the seventh?

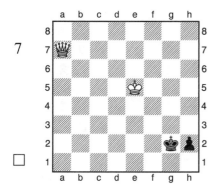

7

Is the white king near enough to win this position?

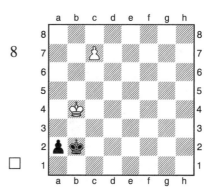

8

Both sides will promote, but how does White then win?

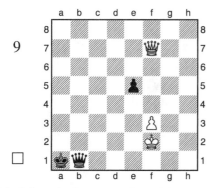

9

Find the winning move for White.

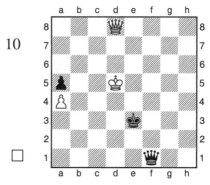

10

The only winning move is a check, but is it 1 ♕g5+, 1 ♕e7+, 1 ♕e8+ or 1 ♕b6+?

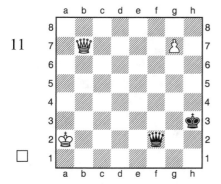

11

White will win with his g7-pawn if only he can stop Black's checks. What's the simplest way to achieve this?

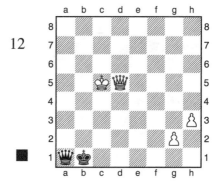

12

White is two pawns up, but Black can draw. How?

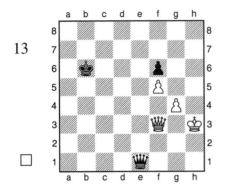

13

On general grounds, what's the best move for White?

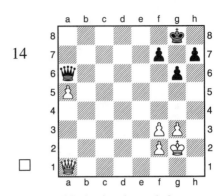

14

What is White's simplest win?

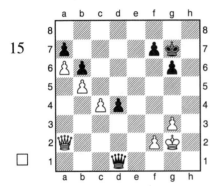

15

Which is the winning move for White?

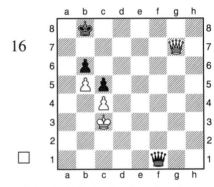

16

Which of White's checks wins the game?

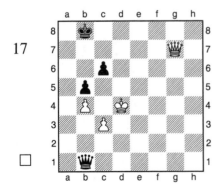

17

Find the only move to win for White.

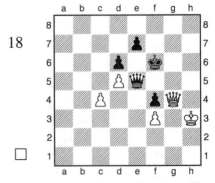

18

Which is best: 1 ♔h2, 1 ♔h4 or 1 ♕c8?

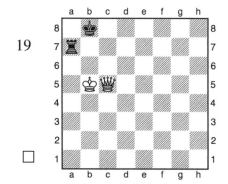

19

Which is better: 1 ♕c6 or 1 ♕d4?

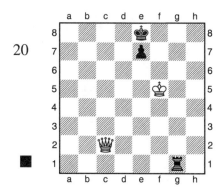

20

Find the only drawing move for Black.

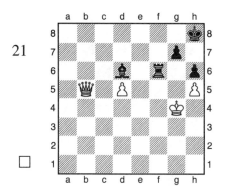

21

Can White win this position?

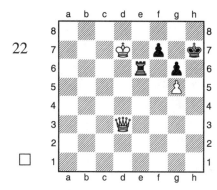

22

How can White break down Black's fortress?

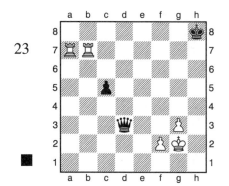

23

Which queen check is correct, 1...♕e4+ or 1...♕d5+?

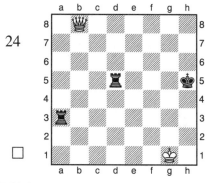

24

Which queen check wins the game?

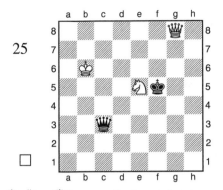

25

$\text{♕}+\text{♘}$ vs ♕ is generally drawn, but there are a few winning positions. Which queen check wins for White?

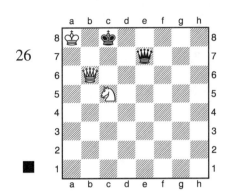

26

Black appears to be in trouble here as White is threatening ♕b8#. Can you find the saving move?

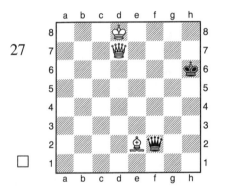

27

Find the only move which wins for White.

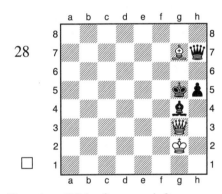

28

How does White force a win?

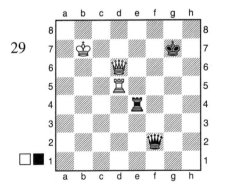

29

If White is to play, how does he win? What is the result if Black is to play?

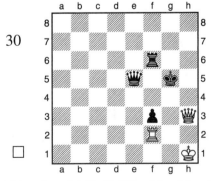

30

White played 1 ♖xf3. Was this a blunder or a brilliancy?

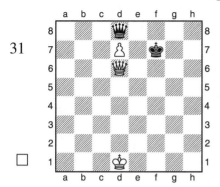

31

Which move is correct: 1 ♔c2, 1 ♔d2 or 1 ♔e2?

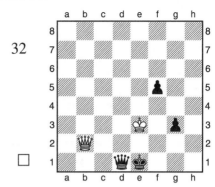

32

Two pawns down, it looks desperate for White. How can he draw?

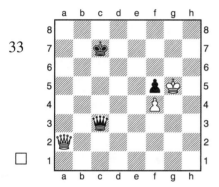

33

On general principles, which move is best: 1 ♔xf5, 1 ♕d5 or 1 ♕a7+?

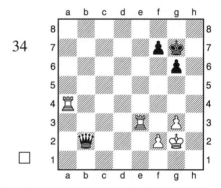

34

White wants to attack the f7-pawn. Should he start with 1 ♖f3, 1 ♖a7 or 1 ♖e7?

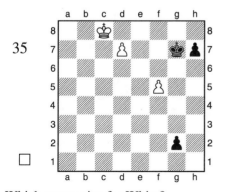

35

Which move wins for White?

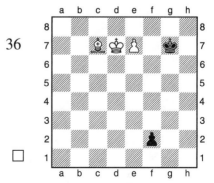

36

Should White play 1 e8♕, or check first by 1 ♗e5+?

Solutions to Queen Ending Exercises

1) White can win. It's a long process but not difficult. The basic idea is to force Black to play his king to e1, blocking the pawn, when White has a free move to bring his own king closer. **1 ♕d6+ ♔c2 2 ♕e5 ♔d2 3 ♕d4+ ♔c2 4 ♕e3 ♔d1 5 ♕d3+ ♔e1 6 ♔b7 ♔f2** (White can repeat the same procedure over and over) **7 ♕d2 ♔f1 8 ♕f4+ ♔g2 9 ♕e3 ♔f1 10 ♕f3+ ♔e1 11 ♔c6 ♔d2 12 ♕f2 ♔d1 13 ♕d4+ ♔c2 14 ♕e3 ♔d1 15 ♕d3+ ♔e1 16 ♔d5 ♔f2 17 ♕d2 ♔f1 18 ♕f4+ ♔g2 19 ♕e3 ♔f1 20 ♕f3+ ♔e1 21 ♔d4 ♔d2 22 ♕d3+** (now the white king is close enough to finish Black off) **22...♔e1 23 ♔e3 ♔f1 24 ♕xe2+ ♔g1 25 ♔f3 ♔h1 26 ♕g2#.**

2) This position is a draw, but the reason is quite subtle. If White plays as in the previous exercise, then to begin with everything is the same: **1 ♕e6+ ♔d2 2 ♕f5 ♔e2 3 ♕e4+ ♔d2 4 ♕f3 ♔e1 5 ♕e3+ ♔f1 6 ♔c7 ♔g2 7 ♕e2 ♔g1 8 ♕g4+ ♔h2 9 ♕f3 ♔g1 10 ♕g3+,** but now a hidden difference appears. When the black king is on the corner side of the f-pawn, there's no need to play the king in front of the pawn. After **10...♔h1!** taking the pawn would stalemate Black, and **11 ♕f3+ ♔g1 12 ♕e3 ♔h1** is a draw since White cannot drive the enemy king to f1, so he has no chance to bring his own king any nearer. Thanks to this stalemate idea, most positions with queen against bishop's pawn on its seventh rank (with the defending king next to the pawn) are drawn.

3) This is a win, even though an f-pawn on the seventh rank normally draws. When the white king is close enough, he can win no matter which pawn Black has. Here White plays **1 ♕a6+! ♔e1 2 ♕a1+ ♔e2 3 ♕b2+** (the idea is to force Black's king to f1 and then play ♔f4; Black tries to avoid blocking his pawn for as long as possible) **3...♔e1 4 ♕b1+ ♔e2 5 ♕e4+ ♔d2 6 ♕f3 ♔e1 7 ♕e3+** (now Black has no choice) **7...♔f1 8 ♔f4 ♔g2 9 ♕e2 ♔g1 10 ♔g3! f1♕** (10...f1♘+ only delays mate by a couple of moves) **11 ♕h2#.**

4) 1...♔e1? 2 ♔e4! f1♕ 3 ♔e3 leaves Black defenceless, while 1...♔e3? 2 ♕g2! ♔e2 3 ♔e4 ♔e1 4 ♔e3 f1♕ 5 ♕d2# also wins for White. The surprising **1...♔f3!** is the only move to draw. f3 is the ideal square for the king because it prevents ♕g2 and avoids having the black king trapped on the edge of the board. After **2 ♕h1+** (Black was threatening to promote, so White must play 2 ♕h1+ or 2 ♕h3+) **2...♔e2 3 ♕g2 ♔e1!** (now playing to e1 is correct, as the queen must be kept away from f1) **4 ♔e4 f1♕** it's a draw. White's queen is attacked so he has no time for ♔e3.

5) Playing pawn endings correctly often requires a knowledge of the queen endings that result if one or both sides promote. Here 1 hxg6? c4 2 g7 c3 3 g8♕ c2 leads to the draw of Exercise 2. White wins by **1 h6! c4 2 h7 c3 3 h8♕ c2** (Black's defence in Exercise 2 depended on stalemate, and having the extra pawn on g6 ruins the stalemate and destroys Black's defence) **4 ♕d4+ ♔e2 5 ♕c3 ♔d1 6 ♕d3+ ♔c1 7 ♔e7 ♔b2** (or 7...g5 8 ♔d6 g4 9 ♔c5 g3 10 ♔c4 g2 11 ♔b3 followed by mate) **8 ♕d4+ ♔b1 9 ♕b4+ ♔a2 10 ♕c3 ♔b1 11 ♕b3+ ♔c1** (after 11...♔a1 White can reply 12 ♕xc2 thanks to the g-pawn) **12 ♔d6** and the king edges closer. Repeating the same manoeuvre over and over leads to a win.

6) This is a draw. Like bishop's pawns, rook's pawns behave differently from the other pawns. Once again, it is stalemate that foils White's winning attempts. The key position arises after **1 ♕g6+ ♔f2 2 ♕h5 ♔g2 3 ♕g4+ ♔f2 4 ♕h3 ♔g1 5 ♕g3+ ♔h1.** Now White faces a problem. He has forced the black king in front of the pawn, but thanks to the edge of the board Black is now stalemated and so White must move his queen again to free the king. This gives him no time to bring his own king closer. The conclusion is that in general a queen beats a pawn on its seventh rank (with no other material, and the defending king next to the pawn) if the pawn is on the b-, d-, e- or g-file, but it's a draw if the pawn is on the a-, c-, f- or h-file.

7) White's king is just near enough to win; indeed, if it were on e6 or d5, for example, the position would be a draw. The winning method is surprising because it involves allowing Black to promote: **1 ♕a2+ ♔g1** (1...♔g3 loses to 2 ♕d5 followed by ♕h1) **2 ♔f4! h1♕ 3 ♔g3** and Black has no useful checks, so it's mate in a few moves.

8) The mating idea from the previous exercise can be used in many other situations. Here it enables White to win an apparently drawn position. **1 c8♕ a1♕ 2 ♕c3+** (White aims to force Black's king to b1 with his queen on the second rank) **2...♔b1** (2...♔a2 3 ♕b3#) **3 ♕d3+ ♔c1** (3...♔b2 4 ♕d2+ ♔b1 5 ♔b3 is a short-cut to the finish) **4 ♕f1+ ♔b2 5 ♕e2+ ♔c1** (Black resists going to b1 for as long as possible...) **6 ♕e1+ ♔b2 7 ♕d2+** (...but now there is no choice) **7...♔b1 8 ♔b3** and mate in a few moves.

9) In a queen ending, you should always be on the lookout for a possible exchange of queens, either by yourself or by your opponent. If one exists, you will need to work out who wins the resulting pawn ending. Here White wins by **1 ♕a7+!** (this forces a queen swap, when White wins because his king can take the e5-pawn) **1...♔b2** (1...♕a2+ 2 ♕xa2+ ♔xa2 3 ♔e3 is also winning) **2 ♕b6+** (2 ♕b7+ and 2 ♕b8+ are just as good) **2...♔c2 3 ♕xb1+ ♔xb1 4 ♔e3 ♔c2 5 ♔e4 ♔d2 6 ♔xe5**.

10) Only one check forces the queen swap that White needs to win. **1 ♕b6+!** (1 ♕e8+? ♔d2!, 1 ♕e7+? ♔d2 and 1 ♕g5+? ♔d3 all let Black off the hook) **1...♔d2** (moving to the f-file allows 2 ♕f6+, while playing to e2 or d3 runs into 2 ♕b5+) **2 ♕b2+!** (2 ♕xa5+? ♔d1 is a draw, as there are few winning chances in ♕+♟ vs ♕ if you have a rook's pawn) **2...♔e3** (2...♔d3 3 ♕b5+) **3 ♕d4+** and next move a check on f6 or c4 swaps queens, after which White runs to take the a5-pawn with his king and promotes his a-pawn.

11) The simplest win is **1 ♕b2!**, which stops any further checks as both **1...♕a7+ 2 ♕a3+** and **1...♕f7+ 2 ♕b3+** interpose with check and so force an exchange of queens. If Black does not check, then White will play 2 ♕b3+ followed by g8♕. The technique of interposing your queen with check is a typical method of stopping a barrage of enemy queen checks.

12) When both sides have queens, the side that is in danger of losing has a powerful drawing weapon at his disposal, namely perpetual check. Here the two connected passed pawns would normally be decisive but giving the correct first check leads to an endless sequence of checks: **1...♕a5+!** (checking on other squares results in the checks drying up; for example, 1...♕c3+? 2 ♔b5 ♕b2+ 3 ♔a4 ♕c2+ and after 4 ♔b4! it's the end, since 4...♕b2+ 5 ♕b3 swaps queens and wins; note, however, that 4 ♕b3+? is a mistake as 4...♕a1! draws by setting up a possible stalemate after 5 ♕xc2) **2 ♔c6 ♕a8+ 3 ♔d6 ♕d8+ 4 ♔e5 ♕g5+ 5 ♔d4** (5 ♔e4 ♕xg2+) **5...♕d2+ 6 ♔c4 ♕a2+** and Black can give checks forever from a2, a5, a8, d8, g8 and so on.

13) Passed pawns are very dangerous in queen endings, especially if they cannot be blocked by the enemy king, so here White should waste no time creating one with **1 g5!**. Not even the World Champion could work out the winning line to the end, but general principles can be useful to help find the right move. Play might continue **1...fxg5 2 f6** (this shows why passed pawns are so dangerous; the only way Black can stop the f-pawn is to put his queen in front, but then the queen is more or less immobilized) **2...♛e6+ 3 ♔g3 ♛f7 4 ♛f5 g4 5 ♔xg4 ♛g8+ 6 ♔h5 ♛h8+ 7 ♔g5 ♛g8+ 8 ♛g6 ♛d5+ 9 ♔h6 ♛h1+ 10 ♔g7** (the checks are at an end since 10...♛b7+ is met by 11 f7+, so Black pins the pawn instead) **10...♛a1 11 ♛f5 ♛b2 12 ♛d5** (now the white queen occupies an active central square) **12...♔c7 13 ♔g6 ♛b6 14 ♛e5+ ♔d8 15 ♔g7 ♛g1+ 16 ♔f8** and now f7 cannot be prevented. Each step forward by the pawn takes many moves to accomplish, but it will get to f8 in the end!

14) In order to remove the blockading queen, White must bring his queen to b6, but after 1 ♛a4 ♔f8 2 ♛b4+ ♔e8 it turns out that 3 ♛b6? only draws as Black's king is close enough to allow a queen swap. It might be that White can still win with a different third move, but it will certainly be difficult. **1 ♛a3!** is the correct move, transferring the queen to b6 without allowing Black's king to move to f8. After **1...h5 2 ♛c5 ♔g7 3 ♛b6 ♛a8 4 a6**, followed by ♛b7, the a-pawn decides the game in White's favour.

15) It looks like Black should be doing well as he already has a passed pawn, but he will lose time because his queen is blocking the pawn. If White acts at once, he can make his own passed pawn and overtake Black in the pawn race. **1 c5! bxc5** (or 1...d3 2 cxb6 d2 3 bxa7 ♛c1 and now the simplest is 4 ♛xd2 ♛xd2 5 a8♛ with two extra passed pawns; it's important that White's promotion prevented ...♛d5+, which might otherwise have led to perpetual check) **2 b6 ♛e1** and now the easiest win is **3 ♛d5** (preventing any counterplay with ...♛e4+) **3...axb6 4 a7** and White will be a queen ahead.

16) If White can take the pawn on b6 with check then he can follow up by taking on c5 and will win with the two extra pawns. The only way to accomplish this is **1 ♛e5+!** (1 ♛g8+? ♔a7 2 ♛h7+ ♔b8! only draws as White can never cross the f-file with checks) **1...♔b7** (1...♔c8 2 ♛e6+ ♔b7 3 ♛c6+ comes to the same thing) **2 ♛d5+ ♔b8 3 ♛d6+** (the queen draws ever nearer) **3...♔b7 4 ♛c6+ ♔a7 5 ♛c7+ ♔a8 6 ♛c8+!** (the key move; 6 ♛xb6? is not check and even allows Black to force stalemate by 6...♛d3+ 7 ♔b2 ♛c2+, etc.) **6...♔a7 7 ♛a6+ ♔b8 8 ♛xb6+ ♔a8 9 ♛xc5**, with a winning position for White.

17) King activity is very important in almost all endings, and queen endings are no exception. Here White wins by advancing his king amongst the enemy pawns. **1 ♔c5! ♛e4** (defending the c6-pawn, at least for the moment) **2 ♔b6** (the king advances further and now White is threatening mate) **2...♛e3+ 3 ♛d4** (the simplest, although 3 ♔xc6 also wins) **3...♛e8** (3...♛xd4+ 4 cxd4 is hopeless for Black, and if the queen moves anywhere else White can win with 4 ♛d8+ or 4 ♛h8+) **4 ♛d6+ ♔a8 5 ♛xc6+** with a winning king and pawn ending.

18) 1 ♛c8? allows Black to force a decisive queen swap by 1...♛f5+! 2 ♛xf5+ ♔xf5 3 ♔h4 ♔e5, winning as in the next line. 1 ♔h4? was played in the game from which this example was taken, and Black replied with the decisive 1...♛e1+!. After 2 ♔h5 (the game finished 2 ♔h3? ♛h1#) 2...♛h1+ 3 ♛h4 ♛xh4+ 4 ♔xh4 ♔e5 5 ♔g4 ♔d4 6 ♔xf4 ♔xc4 7 ♔e4 ♔c5 8 f4 ♔c4 9 f5 ♔c5 Black wins the d5-pawn and the game. **1 ♔h2!** is correct, simply avoiding any queen exchange, after which White should have no trouble drawing.

19) The ending ♕ vs ♖ is almost always a win, but it's not easy and there are some stalemate traps to avoid. An example of that arises after 1 ♕c6?, when Black draws by 1...♖b7+ 2 ♔a6 (if the king moves to the c-file, then ...♖c7 pins the queen) 2...♖a7+ 3 ♔b6 (or else Black just keeps checking on a7 and b7) 3...♖a6+! 4 ♔xa6 stalemate. **1 ♕d4!** looks odd but is the quickest way to win. One line runs **1...♖c7** (1...♖b7+ 2 ♔a6 is essentially the same) **2 ♔b6 ♖b7+ 3 ♔a6**, threatening ♕d8#, and now Black loses his rook in a few moves; for example, **3...♔c8** (or 3...♖c7 4 ♕d8+ ♖c8 5 ♕b6+ ♔a8 6 ♕b7#) **4 ♕h8+ ♔c7 5 ♕g7+**.

20) With ♕ vs ♖+♙, it's often hard to say whether a specific position is a win, but some positions are clearly drawn. In this case, if Black's rook can reach his third rank, the white king will be cut off in the lower part of the board. Then the game is a draw. Hence the drawing idea is **1...♖f1+! 2 ♔e5 ♖f6!** and now the white king can never cross the rank controlled by the rook. Black just moves his rook between d6 and f6, only moving his king if he is checked. White cannot win; for example, **3 ♕c8+ ♔f7 4 ♕g4 ♖d6 5 ♕h5+ ♔f8 6 ♕h8+ ♔f7 7 ♕h7+ ♔f8** and White can only go around in circles.

21) This position is a draw. When playing with lesser pieces against a queen, the key concept is that of a *fortress*. The wide-ranging queen can easily pick off undefended pieces, but if everything is defended and the enemy king is kept out, then the result is often a draw. Here, for example, **1 ♕e8+ ♔h7 2 ♕c8 ♖f4+ 3 ♔h3 ♖f3+ 4 ♔g2 ♖f6 5 ♕e8 ♗f8** shows how powerless White is so long as Black stops the d-pawn from advancing by keeping both his pieces guarding d6.

22) This may look like a fortress, but White can demolish it by giving up his queen to reach the win of Exercise 18 on page 18. **1 ♕h3+** (other moves also win, but this is the simplest) **1...♔g7 2 ♕xe6 fxe6 3 ♔xe6** and White wins; for example, **3...♔g8 4 ♔f6 ♔h7 5 ♔f7 ♔h8 6 ♔xg6 ♔g8 7 ♔h6 ♔h8 8 g6 ♔g8 9 g7** followed by ♔h7.

23) In queen endings, it's important to know when you have perpetual check. Here Black's only hope of saving the game is perpetual check, but he must choose the right check on the first move: **1...♕d5+!** (1...♕e4+? 2 ♔h2 stops the checks and wins) **2 f3** (or 2 ♔h2 ♕h5+ 3 ♔g1 ♕d1+, etc.) **2...♕d2+ 3 ♔h3 ♕h6+ 4 ♔g4 ♕e6+** (4...♕g6+ also draws) **5 ♔f4 ♕f6+ 6 ♔e4 ♕d4+ 7 ♔f5 ♕d5+ 8 ♔g4 ♕e6+** and the position repeats.

24) Having undefended pieces is likely to cause trouble if your opponent has a queen. The queen's ability to fork two pieces means that undefended pieces are rarely safe, especially if the queen has several checks available. If White chooses the correct first check then he can win a rook within a few moves: **1 ♕e8+!** (1 ♕h8+? ♔g4! draws since 2 ♕g8+ is safely met by 2...♖g5, while 1 ♕h2+? ♔g6 also doesn't work) **1...♔g4** (after 1...♔g5 2 ♕g8+ and 1...♔h6 2 ♕e6+ Black loses the d5-rook, and if 1...♔h4 then 2 ♕e4+ as in the main line) **2 ♕e4+ ♔g3 3 ♕g2+!** (not 3 ♕xd5?? ♖a1+ and mate next move) followed by **4 ♕xd5** and White has the decisive material advantage of ♕ vs ♖.

25) After **1 ♕g4+!** (only this surprising check is effective) **1...♔f6** (1...♔xe5 loses the queen to a skewer: 2 ♕g7+) **2 ♕g6+** (2 ♕f4+ ♔e6 3 ♕f7+ is also good) **2...♔e7** the simplest line is **3 ♕f7+ ♔d6 4 ♘c4+**, winning Black's queen.

26) 1...♕e5? allows 2 ♕b7+ ♔d8 3 ♕d7#, while playing for stalemate by 1...♕a7+? doesn't work because 2 ♕xa7 lifts the stalemate. The tactical trick **1...♕d6!** is the only way to draw and since **2 ♕b7+ ♔d8** leads nowhere, White has nothing better than **2 ♕xd6** stalemate.

27) The cunning ambush **1 ♕d2+!** sets up a possible discovered attack by the bishop. After **1...♔g7** (the only move, as 1...♔g6 and 1...♔h7 allow 2 ♗d3+, winning the queen) **2 ♕g5+** (not 2 ♕b2+? ♕f6+) the black king comes under a decisive attack. White wins after **2...♔f8 3 ♕h6+** followed by ♗c4+ or **2...♔h7 3 ♗d3+ ♔h8 4 ♕h6+ ♔g8 5 ♗c4+**, picking up the black queen.

28) Opposite-coloured bishops often lead to a draw when there are no other pieces on the board, but if in addition there are major pieces such as rooks or queens around, the bishops can lend force to an attack. Here White has a beautiful win by **1 ♕h4+!** (1 ♕e3+? ♔g6 lets Black escape) **1...♔f4** (1...♔xh4 2 ♗f6#, 1...♔g6 2 ♕f6# and 1...♔f5 2 ♕f6+ ♔e4 3 ♕d4+ ♔f5 4 ♕e5+ ♔g6 5 ♕f6# all lead to a quick mate) **2 ♕f2+ ♗f3+** (2...♔e4 3 ♕c2+ costs Black his queen, while 2...♔g5 3 ♕f6# is again mate) **3 ♕xf3+ ♔g5 4 ♕g3+ ♔f5 5 ♕d3+** and Black loses his queen.

29) If White is to play, he wins by **1 ♖g5+!** (1 ♕c7+? ♔f6! 2 ♖d6+ ♖e6 and 1 ♕d7+? ♕f7 2 ♖g5+ ♔f8 3 ♖f5 ♖e7 4 ♖xf7+ ♔xf7 don't lead to anything) **1...♔f7** (1...♔h8 2 ♕h6#) **2 ♕g6+ ♔e7 3 ♕xe4+**. With Black to play, **1...♕f7+!** (1...♕b2+? only draws: 2 ♔c7 ♖c4+ 3 ♖c5) wins since White loses his queen after **2 ♕d7 ♖e7, 2 ♔c8 ♖e8+** or **2 ♔c6 ♖e6**. When there are queens and rooks on the board and both kings are exposed, whoever gets the first check usually wins.

30) **1 ♖xf3!** was an excellent move, leading a clear draw (1 ♖f1 is the only other move to draw, but is much more complicated). Then **1...♖h6** (1...♕e1+ 2 ♔h2! ♕e2+ 3 ♕g2+ is also a draw) looks like a winning reply, but the remarkable defence **2 ♖g3+! ♕xg3** (forced, since other moves even lose) **3 ♕xh6+! ♔xh6** forces stalemate.

31) Black cannot move his queen unless he can give check, and if White chooses the right squares for his king he can prevent Black from giving a useful check. **1 ♔c2!** (1 ♔e2? ♕e7+ 2 ♕xe7+ ♔xe7 is a draw at once, while 1 ♔d2? ♕g5+ 2 ♔d3 ♕f5+ 3 ♔d4 ♕f2+ 4 ♔d5 ♕a2+ allows Black to give perpetual check) **1...♔g7** (Black has no checks and can only move his king) **2 ♔d3! ♔f7 3 ♔c4** (the 'staircase' walk by the white king continues) **3...♔g7** (after 3...♕h4+ 4 ♔b5 ♕g5+ 5 ♔a6 White stops the checks and wins by 5...♕d8 6 ♔b7 ♔g7 7 ♕c7) **4 ♔b5 ♔f7** (4...♕g5+ 5 ♔a6 is still winning) **5 ♔c6 ♕a8+ 6 ♔b6 ♕d8+ 7 ♔b7 ♔g7 8 ♕c7** and wins. White's far-advanced passed pawn effectively paralysed Black's queen.

32) Normally Black's two extra pawns would win easily, but here White has the defence **1 ♕b4+ ♔f1 2 ♕f4+ ♔g2** (otherwise Black loses the g-pawn with check) **3 ♕xg3+!** (3 ♕xf5? ♕e1+ 4 ♔d4 ♕f2+ exchanges queens and wins) **3...♔xg3** and amazingly White is stalemated. It's often hard to see stalemates with the king in the middle of the board, as they normally only arise when the king is on the edge of the board or in a corner.

33) 1 ♕xf5? allows perpetual check because White's queen is stuck far away at the edge of the board: 1...♕d3+ 2 ♔g4 ♕g6+ 3 ♔f3 ♕d3+ 4 ♔f2 ♕d4+ 5 ♔g3 ♕d3+. Black also draws after 1 ♕a7+? (this check doesn't help White to centralize his queen) 1...♔d8! (1...♔d6? 2 ♕f7! ♕g3+ 3 ♔xf5 ♕d3+ 4 ♔g5 ♕g3+ 5 ♔h6 ♕h4+ 6 ♔g7 is bad for Black as there are no more checks and then the pawn can advance) 2 ♕f7 ♕g3+ 3 ♔xf5 ♕d3+ 4 ♔g5

♕g3+ 5 ♔h6 ♕h4+ 6 ♔g7 ♕g3+ (6...♕g4+? 7 ♔f8) 7 ♔f8 ♕a3+ and the checks continue. **1 ♕d5!** is the only move to win. A useful general rule for queen endings is that queens are at their most powerful when they occupy the centre of the board. Here centralizing the queen is more important than the immediate capture of Black's pawn. One possible line is **1...♕g7+ 2 ♔xf5** (thanks to the active queen on d5, White can now take the pawn without allowing perpetual check) **2...♕h7+ 3 ♔g4 ♕g6+ 4 ♕g5 ♕e6+ 5 ♔h5** (5 f5? ♕e2+! is perpetual check again after 6 ♔h4 ♕h2+ or 6 ♔f4 ♕d2+) **5...♕h3+ 6 ♔g6 ♕e6+ 7 ♕f6 ♕g4+ 8 ♔f7 ♕h5+ 9 ♔f8** and there are no more checks, so the pawn can advance.

34) Two rooks are often better than a queen because they can gang up on a target and attack it twice, while the queen can only defend it once. Here the target is the f7-pawn, but which is the best way to arrange the rooks? 1 ♖a7? ♕d4!, attacking the a7-rook, is a cunning defence, since 2 ♖ee7 ♕d5+ leads to perpetual check after 3 ♔h2 ♕h5+ 4 ♔g1 ♕d1+ 5 ♔g2 ♕d5+ 6 f3 ♕d2+ 7 ♔h3 ♕h6+. 1 ♖f3? ♕b7 is also safe for Black since the f3-rook is pinned and 2 ♖f4 f5 doesn't achieve anything. **1 ♖e7!** threatens both 2 ♖f4 and 2 ♖aa7, and there's no real defence for Black as he cannot give perpetual check. After **1...♕b5** (hoping for 2 ♖aa7? ♕d5+, but White has a second option) **2 ♖f4 ♕d5+ 3 ♖f3 ♔g8 4 ♖xf7** (liquidating to a winning pawn ending) **4...♕xf7 5 ♖xf7 ♔xf7 6 ♔f3 ♔f6 7 ♔g4 ♔f7 8 ♔g5 ♔g7 9 f4 ♔f7 10 ♔h6 ♔f6 11 g4 ♔f7 12 g5** the g-pawn falls, when White wins easily.

35) Queen endings often arise when both sides promote a pawn. Sometimes you can improve your chances with a preliminary action before the pawns promote. Here 1 d8♕? g1♕ 2 f6+ ♔h6 doesn't win; for example, 3 f7 ♕c5+ 4 ♔b8 ♕b5+ is a draw because the white queen is poorly placed on the edge of the board. White can win by advancing the f-pawn **before** the pawns promote: **1 f6+! ♔h6** (after 1...♔xf6 2 d8♕+ White promotes with check, 1...♔g6 2 d8♕ g1♕ 3 ♕g8+ is a skewer and 1...♔f7 2 d8♕ g1♕ 3 ♕e7+ either mates after 3...♔g8 4 ♕e8# or wins the queen by 3...♔g6 4 ♕g7+) **2 f7** (this is why it is better to check before promoting the d-pawn: White has the option of promoting the f-pawn instead) **2...g1♕** (after 2...♔g7 promoting either pawn wins) **3 f8♕+ ♔h5 4 d8♕** with an easy win for White.

36) This is a more complicated example of a preliminary action before both sides promote. **1 ♗e5+!** (♕+♗ vs ♕ is normally a draw, and after 1 e8♕? f1♕ 2 ♗e5+ ♔h6, for example, White has lots of checks but cannot win) **1...♔h6** (Black cannot allow White to promote with check, so he must move to h6 or h7; however, 1...♔h7 loses to 2 e8♕ f1♕ 3 ♕h5+ ♔g8 4 ♕g6+ ♔f8 5 ♗d6#) **2 ♗f4+!** (after 1 e8♕? f1♕ 2 ♗e5+ ♔h6 White did not have this check, as Black could have simply taken the bishop; that's why White had to give the checks before the pawns promote) **2...♔g7 3 e8♕ f1♕ 4 ♕e7+ ♔g6** (4...♔g8 is the same) **5 ♕g5+ ♔f7** (5...♔h7 6 ♕h6+ ♔g8 7 ♕g6+ and mate in two more moves) **6 ♕f5+ ♔g7** (6...♔g8 7 ♕g6+ again mates) **7 ♗e5+** and White wins the queen.

7 Endgame Tactics

Tactics occur surprisingly often in endings. This chapter shows how mate, stalemate, pawn promotion and many other tactical ideas arise in endings. Staying alert for your own tactical possibilities is a great point-winner, while spotting similar ideas for your opponent can avoid an unnecessary loss. Some of the exercises in this chapter are harder than those earlier in the book. Don't worry if you can't solve them; just play over the solutions and enjoy the tactics.

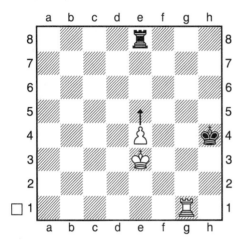

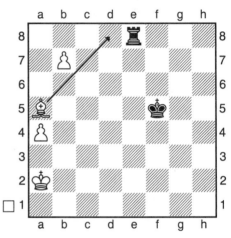

Although mate appears unlikely when there are few pieces left on the board, it is important in many endgame positions. White can only win if he can advance his pawn to the fifth rank, but after the obvious 1 ♔d4 Black plays 1...♖d8+ and keeps checking or attacking the pawn until the king returns to e3. The winning move is **1 e5!**, which looks like a blunder, allowing Black to take the pawn with check, but it's a clever idea to advance the pawn. The point is that 1...♖xe5+ 2 ♔f4 threatens mate by 3 ♖h1# and so wins the black rook. Black has nothing better than **1...♔h5** but now that the pawn is on the fifth rank, White wins by heading for the Lucena position (see Exercise 25 on page 58): **2 ♔e4 ♔h6 3 ♔d5 ♖d8+ 4 ♔c6 ♖e8 5 ♔d6 ♖d8+ 6 ♔e7 ♖d2 7 e6 ♖e2 8 ♔f7 ♖f2+ 9 ♔e8** followed by e7, with the standard Lucena win.

Tactics can often be used to help promote a pawn. Here White must move his bishop so that the a-pawn can advance, but which square is correct? Recall that White cannot win with a dark-squared bishop plus a-pawn if Black can get his king to a8 (see Exercise 25 on page 36). It follows that the obvious 1 ♗c7? ♔e6 2 b8♕ (2 a5 ♔d7 3 ♗f4 ♔c6 is also a draw) 2...♖xb8 3 ♗xb8 ♔d7 4 a5 ♔c8 followed by ...♔b7 and ...♔a8 is only a draw. 1 ♗b6? is also bad as 1...♖b8 wins the b-pawn. The only move to win is the amazing bishop sacrifice **1 ♗d8!!**. The idea is to gain time to allow the a-pawn to advance and support its colleague on b7. With two connected passed pawns running up the board, White is sure to make a queen. After **1...♖xd8 2 a5 ♔e6 3 a6 ♖b8 4 a7 ♖xb7 5 a8♕** White has a decisive material advantage.

96

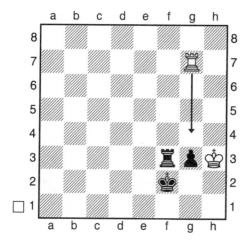

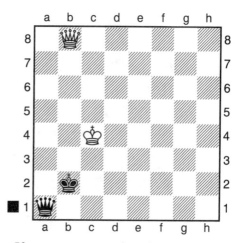

Another common endgame tactic is stalemate, which can be used to save an otherwise hopeless situation. Black threatens 1...♖f8! (intending ...♖h8+) 2 ♖xg3 ♖h8+ 3 ♔g4 ♖g8+ followed by ...♖xg3. White cannot move his rook off the g-file as Black would promote his pawn by ...g2+, so he must move along the g-file. Most moves, such as 1 ♖g5? and 1 ♖g6?, do nothing to counter Black's threat and so lose to 1...♖f8. After 1 ♖g8? ♖f7! White loses the same way. Only 1 ♖g4! works. Then 1...♖a3 is met by 2 ♖g8 since after 2...♖a7 3 ♖f8+ Black loses the pawn. Playing the black rook round to the h-file is only dangerous when the rook stands on the f-file and so prevents a white check. But what happens if Black just goes ahead and tries to execute his threat by 1...♖f8? Then White forces a surprise draw by 2 ♖f4+! ♖xf4 stalemate, explaining why only the rook move to the fourth rank saves the game.

If you are aware of tactical possibilities for your opponent, then you can avoid unnecessary losses. Here Black is in check, but where should he move his king? 1...♔a2? and 1...♔a3? allow 2 ♕b3# and 1...♔c2? 2 ♕h2+ ♔c1 (2...♔b1 is met by the immediate 3 ♔b3) 3 ♕g1+ ♔b2 4 ♕f2+ ♔a3 (4...♔c1 5 ♕e1+ ♔b2 6 ♕d2+ transposes) 5 ♕e3+ ♔b2 6 ♕d2+ ♔b1 (6...♔a3 7 ♕b4+ ♔a2 8 ♕b3#) 7 ♔b3 leads to mate in a few moves (this is similar to Exercise 8 on page 85). The only other move is 1...♔c1!, and this is the way to draw. White can try various checks, but so long as Black responds correctly, White can never reach a winning position; for example, 2 ♕f4+ ♔b1! (once again every other move loses; after 2...♔c2? 3 ♕f2+ or 2...♔b2? 3 ♕d2+ White wins as after 1...♔c2?) 3 ♕f5+ ♔a2! (3...♔b2? still loses, to 4 ♕f2+) and Black draws so long as he keeps his king on b1 or a2, so that checks along the second rank (with the king on a2) or along the b-file (with the king on b1) can be met by ...♕b2.

Exercises

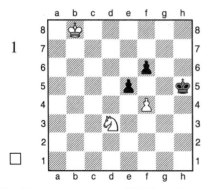

1

Black is trying to swap off White's last pawn. How should White react?

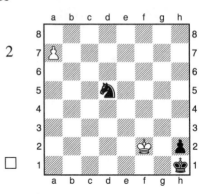

2

Can White (to play) win?

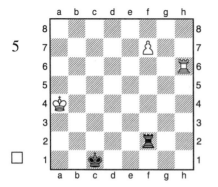

3

Black is playing for stalemate but White has one winning move. Which one?

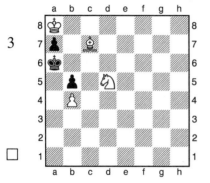

4

White is two pawns up, but his h-pawn is in danger. How does he win?

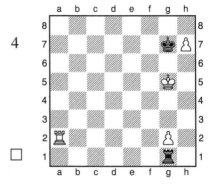

5

How can White win?

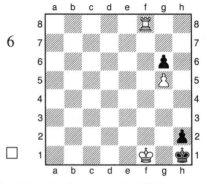

6

Find the winning move for White.

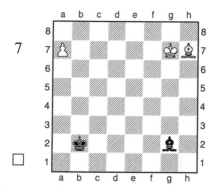

7

How can White ensure the promotion of his pawn?

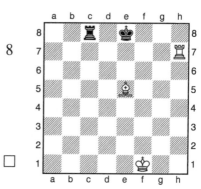

8

How can White use zugzwang to score a quick win?

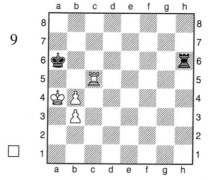

9

Rook and doubled pawns vs rook is usually a draw, but here White can win with a surprise tactic. What should he play?

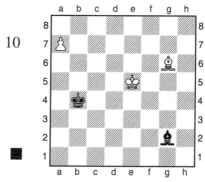

10

Compared to Exercise 7, Black's king is closer to the white pawn. How does this enable him to draw?

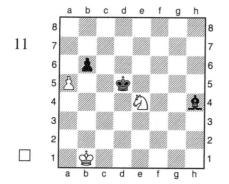

11

How does White force the promotion of his pawn?

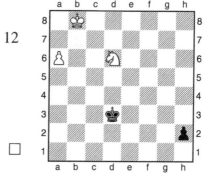

12

How does White win?

99

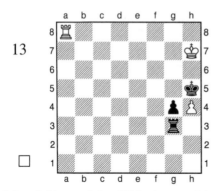

13

Material is equal, but White has a quick win. How?

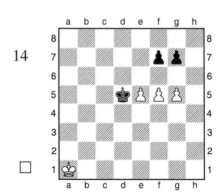

14

How does White create a passed pawn and win?

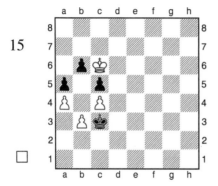

15

The position is symmetrical but White can win. How?

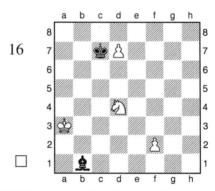

16

If White loses his d7-pawn for nothing, it will be a draw. Can you find the hidden path to victory?

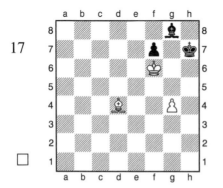

17

Opposite-coloured bishops often mean a draw, but not here! How does White win?

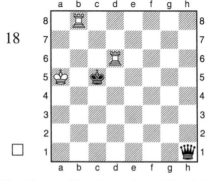

18

Black is attacking the rook on d6 and threatening ...♕a1#, but White can win. How?

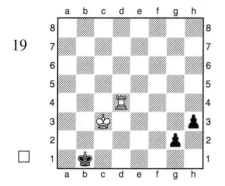

19

How can White use zugzwang to win the game?

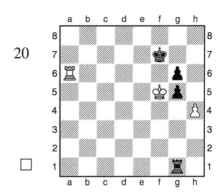

20

White is in check. Can he safely play 1 ♖xg6?

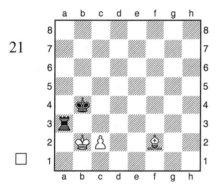

21

Should White play 1 ♗e1+ or 1 ♗c5+?

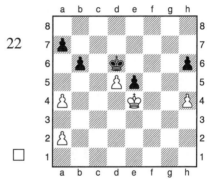

22

Whoever moves his king first will lose a pawn and the game. How can White win?

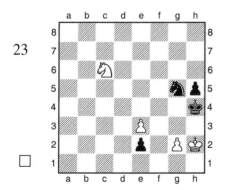

23

Black's pawn is about to promote. How can White save the game?

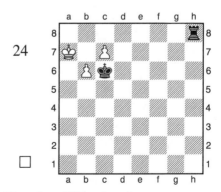

24

How does White draw?

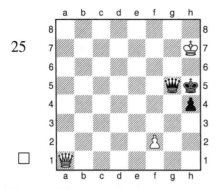

25

How can White mate in six moves with a series of checks?

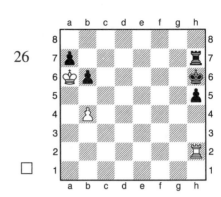

26

It looks hopeless for White since he is two pawns down, yet he can save the game. How?

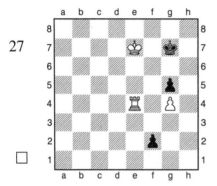

27

Can White save the game?

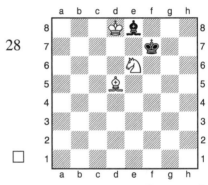

28

Which is the best move: 1 ♘c7+, 1 ♗a2, 1 ♗b3 or 1 ♗c4?

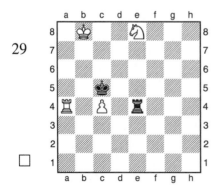

29

Losing White's pawn would lead to a drawn ending of ♖+♘ vs ♖. Which surprising move allows White to win?

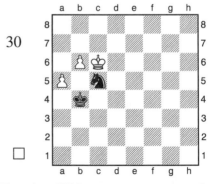

30

How does White promote a pawn and win?

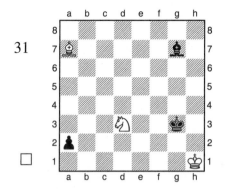

31

How does White draw despite the apparently unstoppable a-pawn?

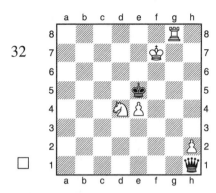

32

White needs something special to win. Can you find it?

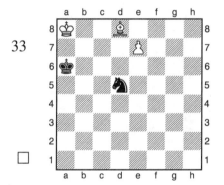

33

Find the best move for White.

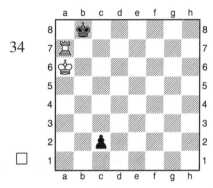

34

The c-pawn appears impossible to stop, but White can draw regardless. How?

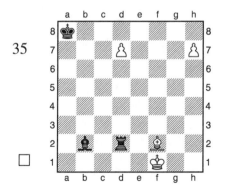

35

How does White promote one of his pawns and win?

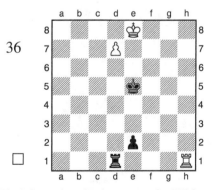

36

Find the only winning move for White.

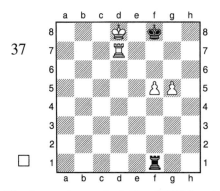

37

The f-pawn is attacked. Should White play 1 f6 or 1 ♖d5?

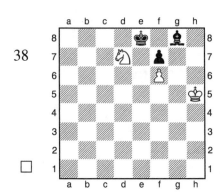

38

Where should White move the attacked knight?

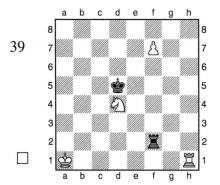

39

White's knight and pawn are both under attack. How does he win?

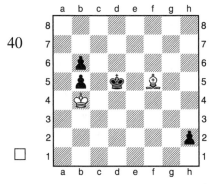

40

How can White draw despite the danger posed by Black's h-pawn?

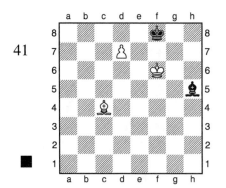

41

Black played 1...♗e8, banking on the stalemate after 2 d8♕ or 2 d8♖. Does this save the game?

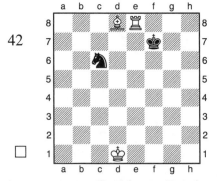

42

Black's plan is 1 ♖h8 ♔g7 2 ♖e8 ♔f7, repeating the position. How can White avoid this and win?

43

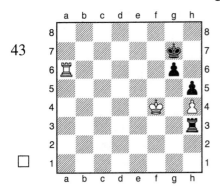

If White loses his pawn for nothing, then he will lose the game. What should he play?

44

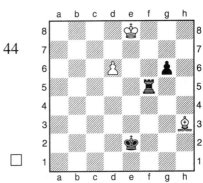

Recall that ♕ vs pawn on f2 is generally a draw. Should White play 1 ♗xf5 or 1 ♗g4+, and why?

45

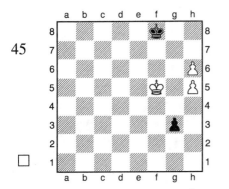

Which move is correct: 1 h7, 1 ♔g6 or 1 ♔f6?

46

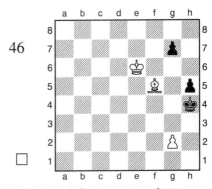

Black plans ...♔g3, meeting ♗h3 by ...g5-g4 and ♗e4 with ...h4-h3. How can White win?

47

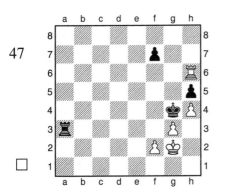

Which move is best: 1 ♖b6, 1 ♖f6 or 1 ♖h7?

48

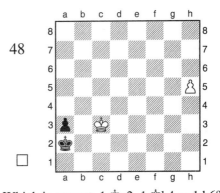

Which is correct: 1 ♔c2, 1 ♔b4 or 1 h6?

Solutions to Endgame Tactics Exercises

1) After 1 f5? ♔g5 White loses the pawn at once, so **1 ♘xe5!** is the only way to keep the pawn. After **1...fxe5 2 fxe5 ♔g6 3 ♔c7! ♔f7** (or 3...♔f5 4 ♔d6) **4 ♔d7** White will promote the e-pawn.

2) White can win, but only one move works. 1 a8♕? and 1 a8♗? are draws by stalemate, while after 1 ♔f1? ♘b6 Black stops the pawn and draws. The sole winning move is **1 a8♖!** followed by mate with 2 ♖a1+.

3) **1 ♗b6!** avoids stalemate and leads to a forced mate after **1...axb6 2 ♘c7#**.

4) 1 ♖a7+? ♔h8 2 g4 is tempting because it keeps both pawns, but 2...♖xg4+! draws because of the stalemate after 3 ♔xg4. The winning line is **1 h8♕+! ♔xh8 2 ♔g6** with the deadly threat of 3 ♖a8#. Even giving up the rook by **2...♖xg2+** only delays mate for a couple of moves: **3 ♔xg2 ♔g8 4 ♖f2 ♔h8 5 ♖f8#**.

5) Just defending the pawn with 1 ♖h7? only draws after 1...♖f5 2 ♔b4 ♔d2 3 ♔c4 ♔e3 followed by ...♔e4, ...♖f1 and then ...♔e5-e6, winning the pawn. White wins by **1 ♖h1+! ♔d2 2 ♖h2!** and the pin deflects the rook, allowing White to promote after **2...♖xh2 3 f8♕**. Then White has the winning material advantage of ♕ vs ♖.

6) Black is currently stalemated. White can lift the stalemate by 1 ♔e2?, but Black replies 1...♔g2 2 ♖f2+ ♔g3 3 ♖f1 ♔g2 4 ♖a1 h1♕ 5 ♖xh1 ♔xh1 6 ♔f3 ♔h2 7 ♔f4 ♔h3 and now 8 ♔e5? ♔g4 9 ♔f6 ♔h5 even loses for White, so he should be content with a draw after 8 ♔f3 ♔h4 9 ♔g2 ♔xg5 10 ♔g3. The correct way to lift the stalemate is **1 ♖f5!**, winning after **1...gxf5 2 g6 f4 3 g7 f3 4 g8♕** (4 g8♗ also wins) **4...f2 5 ♕a8#** (or 5 ♕d5#).

7) White must use his king to help challenge the long diagonal leading to a8. There is no time to lose as Black is threatening to march his king up the board and take White's pawn, so the winning line is **1 ♔f6! ♔c3 2 ♔e5 ♔b4 3 ♗e4** and the pawn will promote.

8) **1 ♗c7!** is the only move to win. There is no immediate threat, but Black is in zugzwang. He must play **1...♖a8** or **1...♔f8** to avoid the immediate capture of his rook, but in both cases White replies **2 ♖h8+** and wins the rook after all.

9) **1 ♖c6+!** (a decoy plus fork combination enables White to swap off into a winning king and pawn ending) **1...♖xc6 2 b5+ ♔b6 3 bxc6 ♔xc6 4 ♔a5!** (4 ♔b4? ♔b6 is a draw – see Exercise 7 on page 17) **4...♔b7 5 ♔b5** (5 b4? ♔a7 is again drawn) **5...♔a7 6 ♔c6** and White wins as in Exercise 6 on page 16.

10) 1...♔c5? is too slow and allows White to win by 2 ♗e4, but the surprising **1...♗a8!** holds White up just long enough to win the a-pawn after **2 ♗e4 ♔c5** (2...♔a5 and 2...♔b5 are just as good) **3 ♗xa8 ♔b6**. Now Black draws since, thanks to his first move, White's bishop is blocking an immediate pawn promotion.

11) White wins by **1 a6** (after 1 axb6? ♔c6 the pawn is lost) **1...♔c6 2 ♘d6!**, a surprising move covering b7 and so threatening 3 a7. Whether or not Black takes the knight, there's no way he can prevent a7 and a8♕.

12) **1 ♘e4!** (1 a7? h1♕ 2 a8♕ ♕xa8+ 3 ♔xa8 is just a draw, but the preliminary knight sacrifice draws Black's king into a bad position) **1...♔xe4** (1...h1♕ loses to 2 ♘f2+, while 1...♔e3 loses to 2 ♘g3 ♔f2 3 a7 ♔xg3 4 a8♕ followed by ♕h1) **2 a7 h1♕** (2...♔f3 3 a8♕+ and 4 ♕h1 is also winning for White) **3 a8♕+** with a decisive skewer.

13) 1 ♔g7? threatens 2 ♖h8#, but after 1...♔xh4 Black avoids the mate and even wins. White can win by playing for mate in a different way: **1 ♖h8! ♔xh4** (or else 2 ♔g7#) **2 ♔g6#**. Playing the rook move first allowed White to keep open the option of moving to g7 or g6 with his king.

14) Black is threatening to take all White's pawns with his king. The only way to save the game is also the only way to win: **1 e6! fxe6** (after 1...♔d6 2 exf7 ♔e7 3 g6 White wins with the two extra pawns, although it still requires a little work: 3...♔f8 4 ♔b2 ♔e7 5 ♔c3 ♔f8 6 ♔d4 ♔e7 7 ♔e5 ♔f8 8 f6 gxf6+ 9 ♔e6! ♔g7 10 ♔e7 and White wins) **2 f6! gxf6 3 g6!** (3 gxf6? ♔d6 4 ♔b2 e5 5 ♔c3 ♔e6 6 ♔d3 ♔xf6 7 ♔e4 is enough to draw, but it doesn't win) and the g-pawn will promote, as the pawn on e6 prevents the black king from catching the pawn.

15) The obvious start is **1 ♔xb6 ♔xb3** (1...♔b4 2 ♔c6 ♔xb3 3 ♔b5! is the same as the main line), but now both 2 ♔xc5? ♔xa4 3 ♔b6 ♔b4 4 c5 a4 and 2 ♔xa5? ♔xc4 3 ♔b6 ♔b4 4 a5 c4 lead to a drawn ending of ♕ vs ♕. However, White wins with the cunning move **2 ♔b5!**, putting Black in zugzwang. After **2...♔c3 3 ♔xc5** or **2...♔a3 3 ♔xa5** White wins a pawn for nothing and promotes the resulting passed pawn.

16) White wins by **1 ♔b2!** and, surprisingly, the bishop is lost wherever it moves: **1...♗e4 2 ♘e6+ ♔xd7 3 ♘c5+, 1...♗g6 2 ♘e6+ ♔xd7 3 ♘f8+, 1...♗h7 2 ♘e6+ ♔xd7 3 ♘f8+** or **1...♗d3 2 ♘e6+ ♔xd7 3 ♘c5+**. With so many squares apparently available, it's astonishing that the bishop can be trapped.

17) Despite the limited material, White can force mate in three moves: **1 g5!** (confining the king) **1...♔h8 2 g6 fxg6** (or 2...♗h7 3 ♔xf7#) **3 ♔xg6#**.

18) White wins by **1 ♖d1!**, a brilliant move which has multiple points: the queen's path to a1 is blocked so that Black has no useful checks, the queen is attacked and 2 ♖c8+ is an additional threat. After **1...♕xd1 2 ♖c8+** followed by ♖d8+ the skewer wins the queen, while **1...♕h3 2 ♖c8+!** (anyway) **2...♕xc8 3 ♖c1+** is also a decisive skewer.

19) The pawns appear dangerous, but White can exploit the bad position of Black's king by **1 ♖d1+!** (after 1 ♔b3?? g1♕ Black prevents the mate on d1 and wins) **1...♔a2 2 ♖g1!**, putting Black in a deadly zugzwang. His only two legal moves both lead to disaster: **2...♔a3 3 ♖a1#** and **2...h2 3 ♖xg2+** followed by ♖xh2, winning both pawns.

20) **1 ♖xg6!** is best and indeed the only move to draw. If instead White moves his king, then Black replies 1...gxh4 and wins with his two connected passed pawns. Taking on g6 can be met by **1...♖f1+**, which looks like a big problem as White now loses his rook, but after **2 ♔xg5 ♖g1+ 3 ♔h5!** White springs his surprise. The rook falls, but after **3...♖xg6** it is stalemate.

21) 1 ♗c5+? ♔xc5 2 ♔xa3 ♔c4 3 ♔b2 ♔b4 is only a draw – see Exercise 5 on page 16. Instead **1 ♗e1+!** is the winning move, so that after **1...♔a4 2 ♗c3** the rook is trapped. Black is now in zugzwang and to avoid losing a whole rook he must play **2...♖xc3**, but then White wins by **3 ♔xc3 ♔b5 4 ♔d4** (4 ♔b3 ♔c5 5 ♔c3 retains the win but loses time since 5...♔b5 repeats the position) **4...♔c6 5 ♔c4** and this king and pawn ending is a win.

22) White must be very careful to ensure that Black is forced to move his king first. 1 a3? h5 2 a5 bxa5 3 a4 a6 and 1 a5? bxa5 2 h5 (or 2 a3 a4 3 h5 a5) 2...a4 3 a3 a5 both lead to White having to move his king, after which he loses the d-pawn and the game. **1 h5!** is the way to do it. Then White wins: **1...a6** (1...a5 2 a3 is even easier) **2 a5!** (the key move; 2 a3? is wrong due to 2...a5) **2...bxa5** (or 2...b5 3 a3) **3 a4** and Black must move his king. White won because his unmoved a-pawn had the option of advancing either one or two squares.

23) Surprisingly, the drawing method involves forcing Black to promote: **1 ♘d4!** (1 ♘e7? also threatens perpetual check, but there is no threat to take the e-pawn, so Black can win by 1...♔g4!) **1...e1♕** (there is nothing better) **2 ♘f5+ ♔g4 3 ♘h6+ ♔h4 4 ♘f5+** with a draw by perpetual check.

24) The position looks very bad for White, as 1 b7? ♔xc7 and 1 ♔a6? ♖a8# lose at once, but he has an amazing way to save the game: **1 c8♕+! ♖xc8 2 b7 ♖c7** (the only way to prevent 3 b8♕) **3 ♔a8! ♖xb7** stalemate.

25) Endings with queens give rise to mating ideas more often than other endings. Here the bad position of Black's king on the edge of the board provides White with a wonderful opportunity to force mate: **1 ♕d1+** (first White brings his queen to the best position with a series of checks) **1...♔g4 2 ♕d5+ ♔g5 3 ♕f3+ ♔g4** (Black's moves are all forced) **4 ♕f7+** (surprisingly, the win involves forcing the black king away from the edge of the board) **4...♔g5 5 f4+!** (now Black must block in his own king) **5...♕xf4 6 ♕g6#**.

26) **1 b5!** (it's normally not a good idea to block in your own king, but here it sets up the stalemate threat of 2 ♖xh5+) **1...♔g6** (there's no good way to meet the threat; for example, 1...♔g7 2 ♖g2+ ♔f7 3 ♖f2+ ♔e7 4 ♖e2+ ♔f8 5 ♖e8+ with same 'rampant rook' idea) **2 ♖g2+** (2 ♖xh5? ♖xh5 lifts the stalemate) **2...♔f6 3 ♖f2+ ♔e5 4 ♖e2+ ♔d4 5 ♖d2+ ♔c3 6 ♖c2+** with perpetual check or stalemate.

27) Even though White cannot stop the pawn promotion, he can still draw with the surprising **1 ♔d7!** (1 ♖e5? f1♕ 2 ♖xg5+ ♔h6 3 ♖h5+ ♔g6 is lost as Black can easily win the g4-pawn with his queen, leading to a winning position with ♕ vs ♖) **1...f1♕** (there is nothing better) **2 ♖e7+ ♔f6 3 ♖e6+ ♔f7 4 ♖e7+ ♔f8 5 ♖e8+** and White gives perpetual check along the e-file. The king had to move to d7 on the first move to ensure that e6, e7 and e8 were all defended by the king.

MINED SQUARE

108

28) Just as there are many ways you can save a game using stalemate, you must also be aware of possible stalemate traps set by the opponent. Here 1 ♘c7+ ♔f8! 2 ♘xe8? is stalemate, although White could still win by 2 ♘e6+, repeating the position. 1 ♗c4? ♗b5! and 1 ♗b3? ♗a4! both let Black escape by attacking the white bishop. **1 ♗a2!** puts Black in zugzwang and is the only move to win. Now Black is helpless, as he cannot move his bishop to attack its white counterpart. After **1...♗c6** or **1...♗b5** White plays **2 ♘d4+**, while **1...♗a4** runs into **2 ♘c5+**. In every case Black loses his bishop.

29) White cannot save his pawn directly, but the sacrifice **1 ♘d6!** leads to a deadly discovered attack: **1...♔xd6** (if Black does not take the knight, White keeps his pawn) **2 c5+ ♔d5** (or else the rook is lost) **3 ♖xe4 ♔xe4 4 c6** and the pawn promotes.

30) White wins by giving up one pawn to promote the other: **1 b7! ♘xb7 2 a6!** (2 ♔xb7? ♔xa5 is only a draw) **2...♘a5+** (the only chance of stopping the pawn) **3 ♔c7!** and now promotion cannot be stopped. Note that White cannot play his king to a different square, since 3 ♔b6? ♘c4+ followed by ...♔a5 and ...♘b6 draws, while 3 ♔d7? ♘c4 also allows the knight to reach b6.

31) **1 ♗d4!** (White is playing for stalemate) **1...♗xd4 2 ♘c1** and now White is attacking the pawn, so Black is forced to promote. However, **2...a1♕** and **2...a1♖** give stalemate, and **2...a1♘ 3 ♘e2+**, winning the bishop, is also a draw.

32) It's not obvious that Black is doomed by the poor position of his queen. **1 ♖g1!** is the surprise move that seals Black's fate. The queen is attacked, and wherever it moves White wins it with a fork. After **1...♕xh2 2 ♘f3+** or **1...♕xg1 2 ♘f3+** Black loses the queen at once, and **1...♕xe4 2 ♖e1!** ♔xd4 (2...♕xe1 3 ♘f3+ ♔f4 4 ♘xe1 ♔g4 5 ♔g6 ♔h3 6 ♘f3 is winning since after 6...♔g2 7 h4 the pawn will promote) **3 ♖xe4+ ♔xe4 4 ♔g6!** (4 h4? ♔f5! is only a draw) **4...♔f4 5 h4 ♔g4 6 h5** also wins for White.

33) In the endgame, you must take care even in apparently simple positions. Black is attacking the pawn, so it must promote, and what could be more obvious than 1 e8♕? with an extra queen? However, this only draws due to 1...♘c7+! (forking king and queen) 2 ♗xc7 with stalemate. 1 e8♗? is also wrong (in general, two bishops beat a lone knight) as 1...♘c7+! 2 ♗xc7 is still stalemate. 1 e8♘? ♔b5 is drawn as ♗+♘ vs ♘ is almost always a draw. **1 e8♖!** is correct, avoiding the stalemate while giving White enough extra material to win.

34) White cannot prevent Black from promoting his pawn, but he can save the game by aiming for stalemate: **1 ♖b7+ ♔c8** (1...♔a8? loses to 2 ♖c7) **2 ♖b5!** (in general, a lone queen beats a lone rook, but not here) **2...c1♕ 3 ♖c5+! ♕xc5** stalemate.

35) The b2-bishop is preventing the h-pawn from promoting, while the rook on d2 does the same for the d-pawn. By playing **1 ♗d4!** White threatens to promote both pawns and Black can only stop one. After **1...♗xd4** (or 1...♖xd4 2 h8♕+) **2 d8♕+ ♔b7 3 h8♕ ♗xh8 4 ♕xd2** White wins easily.

36) 1 d8♕? ♖xd8+ 2 ♔xd8 ♔e4 3 ♔d7 ♔e3 4 ♔d6 ♔d2 is only a draw, but White can win with the surprising **1 ♖e1! ♖xe1** (after 1...♖xd7 2 ♔xd7 or 1...♔f4 2 ♖xe2 White wins easily) **2 d8♕**. White will win the e-pawn, since any move by the black rook is met by ♕e7+ followed by ♕xe2, while if Black moves his king then White plays ♕d2 and wins the pawn in any case. Then White will have a standard ♕ vs ♖ win.

109

37) In order to win, White must avoid a devilish stalemate trap. The obvious 1 f6? is a mistake due to 1...♖f5! 2 ♖g7 (the only move to avoid losing a pawn) 2...♖xf6! 3 gxf6 stalemate. **1 ♖d5!** is correct and should win with careful play; for example, **1...♖g1 2 f6 ♔f7 3 ♖d7+ ♔f8 4 ♖g7 ♖f1 5 ♔c7!** and White will eventually hide his king on g6, freeing the rook and winning. Note that 5 ♔d7? is wrong due to 5...♖xf6! 6 gxf6 stalemate.

38) A draw would be certain once Black plays ...♗h7 and gets his bishop out. The only way to prevent this move is the crazy-looking **1 ♘f8!**, but amazingly it wins! After **1...♔xf8 2 ♔h6** (Black is in zugzwang and must allow the white king in) **2...♔e8** (2...♗h7 3 ♔xh7 is similar) **3 ♔g7 ♔d7** (Black's bishop cannot be saved) **4 ♔xg8 ♔e6 5 ♔g7** Black is again in zugzwang and must surrender his pawn. This is a marvellous demonstration of the power of zugzwang.

39) White can only win with a cunning double sacrifice: **1 ♘f5!** (White sacrifices his knight to draw Black's rook onto the same rank as the king) **1...♖xf5 2 ♖h5** (next White uses a pin to deflect the black rook away from the f-file) **2...♖xh5 3 f8♕** and White has a decisive material advantage.

40) **1 ♗c8!** (first White tries for a skewer, aiming to meet 1...h1♕ with 2 ♗b7+; since 2 ♗b7+ is a threat in any case, Black's reply is forced) **1...♔c6 2 ♗g4!** (this is White's cunning idea: now that Black's king is covering b5, White can play for stalemate) **2...h1♕** (there's nothing better, since after 2...h1♗ 3 ♗e2 White wins the b5-pawn, with an easy draw) **3 ♗f3+ ♕xf3** stalemate.

41) Despite Black's clever defence, White can still win by choosing the correct under-promotion. **1...♗e8 2 d8♗!** (2 d8♘? is a good try, with the idea that 2...♗h5? loses to 3 ♘e6+, either mating after 3...♔e8 4 ♗b5# or winning the bishop after 3...♔g8 4 ♘f4+, but Black can save the game by 2...♗a4! 3 ♘e6+ ♔e8 and now there is no mate) **2...♗h5** (2...♗f7 is met not by 3 ♗xf7? stalemate but by 3 ♗e7+ and only then ♗xf7+; alternatively, 2...♗a4 3 ♗f7 mates next move by 4 ♗e7#) **3 ♗e7+ ♔e8 4 ♗b5#**.

42) White wins by **1 ♖h8! ♔g7** (if Black does not attack the rook then White moves his bishop and wins with the extra rook) **2 ♗f6+!** (a temporary sacrifice leading to a decisive skewer) **2...♔xf6 3 ♖h6+** followed by ♖xc6.

43) White must not play 1 ♔g5? ♖g3+ 2 ♔f4 ♖g4+, when the h-pawn falls, nor 1 ♖a7+? ♔h6 and again White loses his last pawn. The brilliant defence which saves the game is **1 ♖a4!!** **♖xh4+** (1...♔h6 2 ♔e5 allows White to save his pawn, when the result should be a draw) **2 ♔g5** and Black has no good move: **2...♖xa4** is stalemate, **2...♖h1 3 ♖a7+ ♔f8 4 ♔xg6** is an easy draw, and **2...♖g4+ 3 ♖xg4 hxg4 4 ♔xg4** is a drawn king and pawn ending.

44) The first step is to understand why 1 ♗xf5? doesn't win. Black replies 1...gxf5 2 d7 f4 3 d8♕ f3 4 ♕e7+ (if White does not check then Black plays ...f2 with a draw, but this is his only check) 4...♔f1!. Now there are no more checks and White cannot prevent ...f2, with a draw as in Exercise 2 on page 84. The 'in-between check' **1 ♗g4+!** leaves Black with no good square for his king; for example, moving to the d-file allows White to promote with check. The other king moves also lose; for example, **1...♔e3 2 ♗xf5 gxf5 3 d7 f4 4 d8♕ f3 5 ♕g5+** and White wins as the pawn cannot advance to f2; for example, **5...♔e2 6 ♕e5+** (with the pawn on f3, once White gets a sequence of checks he is sure to win) **6...♔d2 7 ♕f4+ ♔e2**

8 ♕e4+ ♚f2 9 ♚f7 and so on, while after **1...♚f1 2 ♗xf5 gxf5 3 d7 f4 4 d8♕ f3 5 ♕d3+** and **1...♚e1 2 ♗xf5 gxf5 3 d7 f4 4 d8♕ f3 5 ♕a5+** White wins much as after 1...♚e3.

45) White appears lost, as Black's pawn cannot be stopped while Black's king can cope with White's h-pawns. However, there is a remarkable stalemate draw by **1 ♚f6!** (1 h7? ♚g7 is hopeless for White, while after 1 ♚g6? ♚g8 2 h7+ ♚h8 3 ♚h6 g2 White must move his king, after which Black promotes with check and wins) **1...♚g8** (forced, as White threatened h7) **2 ♚g6 g2** (2...♚h8 3 h7 g2 4 ♚h6 is the same) **3 h7+ ♚h8 4 ♚h6** and now **4...g1♕** and **4...g1♖** are stalemate, while other promotions leave Black without enough material to win.

46) 1 ♗h3! (1 ♚e5? is too slow and allows Black to draw with 1...♚g3: 2 ♗h3 g5 followed by ...g4, or 2 ♗e4 h4 followed by ...h3) **1...g5** (if Black changes plan with 1...♚g5 then White wins using his extra piece; for example, 2 ♚e5 ♚h6 3 ♚f4 g5+ 4 ♚f5 g4 5 ♗xg4 hxg4 6 ♚xg4 ♚g6 7 g3 with a win as in Exercise 7 on page 17) **2 ♚f5 g4 3 ♚f4!** (in a surprising twist, White sacrifices his bishop and plays for mate) **3...gxh3** (3...g3 4 ♚f3 is also a win) **4 g3#**.

47) 1 ♖f6? threatens both 2 ♖f4# and 2 f3+, but Black has the stunning reply 1...♖xg3+! 2 fxg3 stalemate. 1 ♖b6? is bad for a more subtle reason: Black replies 1...f6!, intending ...♚f5-g6, with a likely draw, and if 2 ♖xf6 then 2...♖xg3+! still draws even though Black no longer has his f-pawn. **1 ♖h7!** is the best of the three moves (1 ♖h8! is equally good). The two threats are 2 ♖g7+ ♚f5 3 ♖g5+ and 2 f3+ ♚f5 (2...♖xf3 3 ♖g7+ wins the rook) 3 ♖xh5+, in both cases winning the h-pawn. Black cannot meet the two threats and so loses another pawn. With two extra pawns, White should win without much trouble.

48) Of the three moves, 1 h6?? is worst and even loses to 1...♚b1 2 h7 a2 3 h8♕ a1♕+, as the skewer wins White's queen. 1 ♚c2? is second best and leads to a draw after 1...♚a1 2 h6 a2 3 h7 stalemate. The winning line is **1 ♚b4! ♚b2** (or else Black loses his pawn) **2 h6 a2 3 h7 a1♕** (Black promotes first but still loses due to the poor position of his king and queen) **4 h8♕+ ♚b1** (after 4...♚a2 5 ♕a8+ White wins in similar fashion) **5 ♕h1+** (this type of win is familiar from Exercise 8 on page 85) **5...♚b2** (5...♚a2 6 ♕d5+ ♚b1 7 ♕d1+ ♚b2 8 ♕d2+ ♚b1 9 ♚b3 is even quicker) **6 ♕g2+** (the queen can zigzag closer) **6...♚c1 7 ♕f1+ ♚b2 8 ♕e2+ ♚c1 9 ♕e1+ ♚b2 10 ♕d2+ ♚b1 11 ♚b3** with mate in a few moves.

UNDERPROMOTION

111

8 Test Papers

Everything you have learnt so far will be put to the test in this final section. The eight test papers cover every type of ending from the first seven chapters. Most of them depend on ideas developed earlier in the book, so I hope that you were paying attention! The first test is a warm-up with four positions, and the remaining tests all have six positions. The difficulty of each position is indicated by stars next to the diagram, with one star being the easiest and five stars the hardest. All the tests apart from the first have roughly the same level of difficulty.

The text under each diagram explains what you need to do, usually to find a win or draw, although there are some multiple-choice questions. You should write down your answers and then compare them with the solutions (which start on page 120). There you will be awarded points according to the difficulty of the position and how well you answered. Unless stated otherwise, you must find all the moves given in **bold** in the solutions to qualify for the points.

Keep a record of your scores and add them to the score-chart on page 127. Good luck!

Test Paper 1

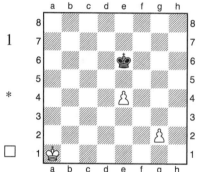

How does White win?

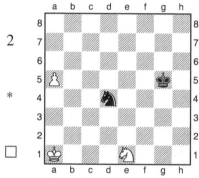

Find the winning move for White.

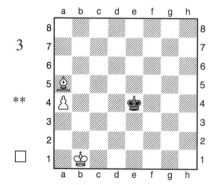

How does White win?

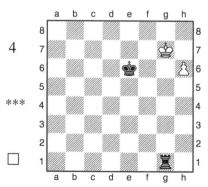

How should White answer Black's check?

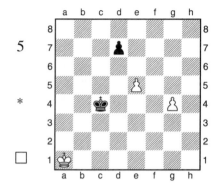

5

*

□

How does White win?

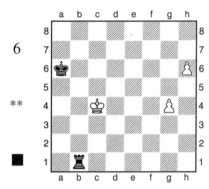

6

**

■

Which move wins for Black?

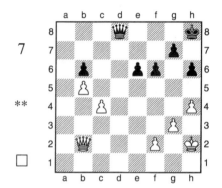

7

**

□

Find a clear-cut win for White.

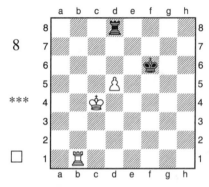

8

***

□

Find the only winning move for White.

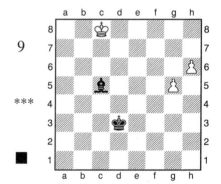

9

***

■

Which move draws for Black?

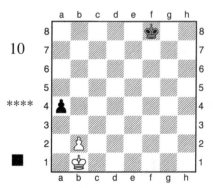

10

****

■

Black continued 1...a3. Should White reply
2 bxa3, 2 b3 or 2 b4?

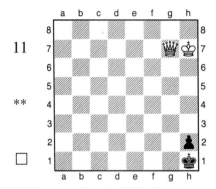

11

**

□

Which move wins for White?

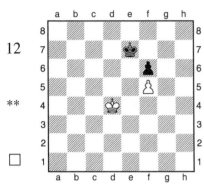

12

**

□

Should White play 1 ♔c5 or 1 ♔d5?

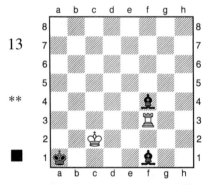

13

**

■

Both bishops are under attack, and ♖a3# is a threat. How can Black save the game?

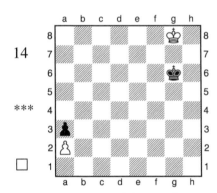

14

***

□

Should White play 1 ♔f8 or 1 ♔h8?

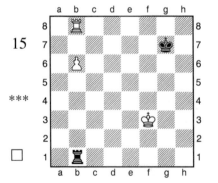

15

***

□

Should White play 1 b7, 1 ♔e3 or 1 ♔e4?

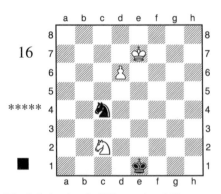

16

*****

■

Black is in check. Where should he move his king?

Test Paper 4

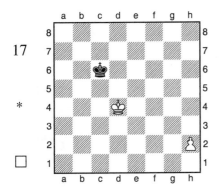

17

*

Which move wins for White?

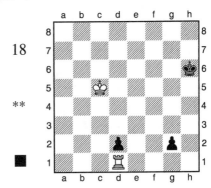

18

**

How can Black draw?

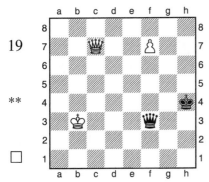

19

**

Where should White move his king?

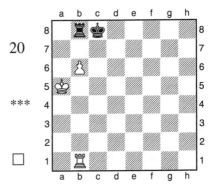

20

***

Is the best move 1 ♔b5, 1 ♖c1+ or 1 ♖h1?

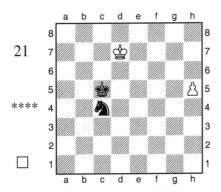

21

****

Find the winning move for White.

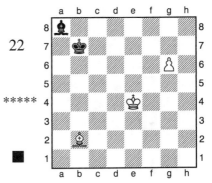

22

*****

Find the drawing continuation for Black.

Test Paper 5

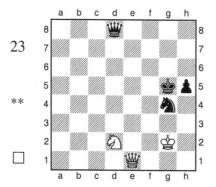

23

**

How can White win quickly?

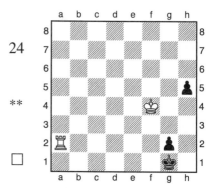

24

**

Should White play 1 ♔f3 or 1 ♔g3?

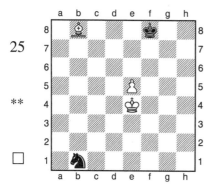

25

**

How does White win?

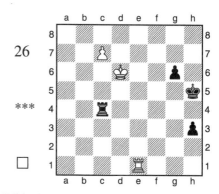

26

***

White is a pawn down, but he can win. How?

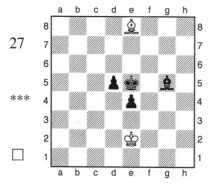

27

***

Find the only move for White to draw.

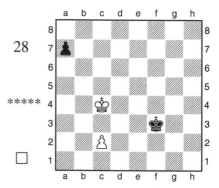

28

*****

What should White play: 1 ♔b5, 1 ♔d5 or 1 ♔d4?

Test Paper 6

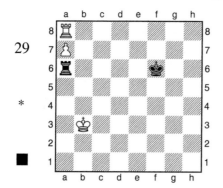

29

*

■

How does Black draw?

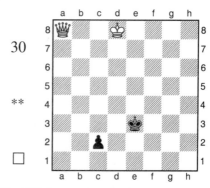

30

**

□

Find White's only winning move.

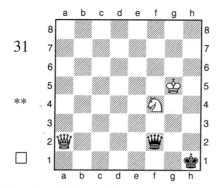

31

**

□

How does White win?

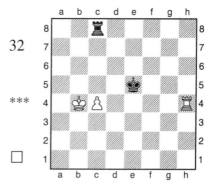

32

***

□

What is the winning move for White?

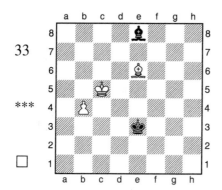

33

***

□

Which move wins for White?

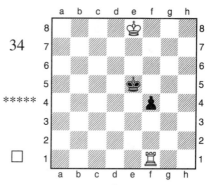

34

*****

□

Should White play 1 ♔d7, 1 ♔e7 or 1 ♔f7?

Test Paper 7

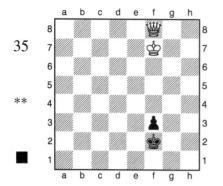

35

**

■

How does Black draw?

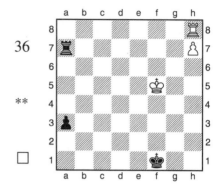

36

**

□

How does White win?

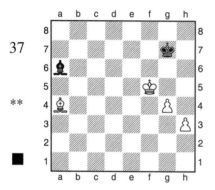

37

**

■

How does Black draw despite being two pawns down?

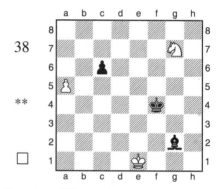

38

**

□

How does White win?

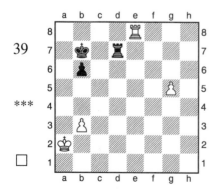

39

***

□

Find the winning move for White.

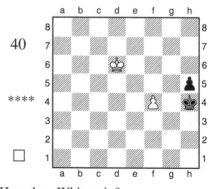

40

****

□

How does White win?

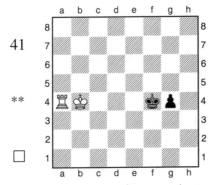

41

**

□

Should White play 1 ♔c3+, 1 ♔c5+ or 1 ♖a8?

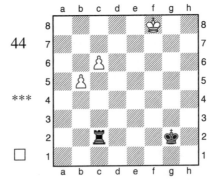

42

**

□

How can White win the knight and the game?

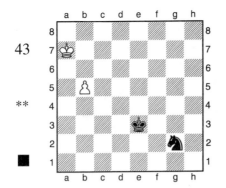

43

**

■

How can Black draw?

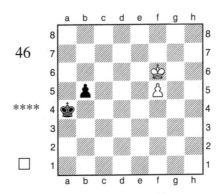

44

***

□

Black is threatening to play ...♖c5 followed by ...♖xb5. How does White win?

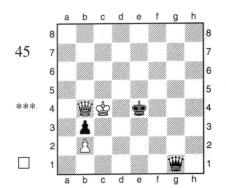

45

***

□

Which move leads to the exchange of queens and a win for White?

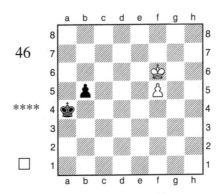

46

****

□

Find the winning line for White.

Solutions to Test Papers

Test Paper 1

1) There is a danger White will lose both pawns so he must use the pawns to support one another: **1 g4! ♔e5** (1...♔f6 2 ♔b2 is also a win as 2...♔e5 is met by 3 g5 and 2...♔g5 by 3 e5) **2 g5!** and Black cannot take on e4 because the g-pawn promotes, so White has time to bring his king up and win. (1 point)

2) 1 ♘f3+! (everything else is too slow; for example, 1 a6? ♘c6 2 ♔b2 ♔f5 3 ♔b3 ♔e5 4 ♔a4 ♔d6 5 ♔b5 ♔c7 with a comfortable draw) **1...♘xf3 2 a6** and the pawn cannot be stopped. This is an example of deflection, which arises quite often in knight endings. (1 point)

3) The ending of rook's pawn plus wrong bishop against lone king is a draw if the black king can reach a8, so White must prevent this at all costs. The only move to succeed is **1 ♗d8!** (1 ♗c7? ♔d5 2 a5 ♔c6 doesn't work because White must now move his bishop, after which Black can play ...♔b7; 1 ♗b6? fails because of 1...♔d5 2 a5 ♔c6, when 3 a6 loses the bishop) **1...♔d5 2 a5 ♔c6 3 a6** and Black is in zugzwang. He must move his king away, allowing White to promote his pawn. (2 points)

4) 1 ♔h7? loses to 1...♔f7 2 ♔h8 ♖g8+ 3 ♔h7 ♖g6 4 ♔h8 ♖xh6# and 1 ♔h8? ♔f6 also loses since 2 h7 (2 ♔h7 ♔f7 is the same as 1 ♔h7?) 2...♖a1 3 ♔g8 ♖a8# mates. **1 ♔f8!** is the only way to draw. Then **1...♖h1** (1...♔f6 2 h7 ♖h1 3 ♔g8 and 1...♖f1+ 2 ♔g7 don't help Black) **2 ♔g7 ♔e7 3 h7 ♖g1+ 4 ♔h8!** is a draw as Black must lift the stalemate by playing the rook along the first rank, after which White just replies ♔g7. Not, however, 4 ♔h6? ♔f7! 5 h8♘+ (5 h8♕ ♖h1+ wins the queen) 5...♔f6 6 ♔h7 ♖g4, winning the knight. (2 points for finding **1 ♔f8!** and 1 extra for seeing up to **4 ♔h8!**)

Test Paper 2

5) A preliminary pawn sacrifice blocks the line from c4 to g8, which the black king needs to catch the g-pawn: **1 e6! dxe6 2 g5 ♔d5 3 g6** wins. (1 point)

6) 1...♖g1! wins because Black threatens to take the g4-pawn with check. After **2 ♔d5 ♖xg4**, followed by ...♖h4, Black takes the other pawn as well. Note that 1...♖h1? 2 ♔d5 ♖xh6 3 ♔e5 allows White to draw; for example, 3...♔b6 4 g5 ♖h1 5 g6 ♔c7 6 g7 ♖g1 7 ♔f6 ♔d7 8 ♔f7 ♖f1+ 9 ♔g6 (9 ♔g8? loses to 9...♔e7 10 ♔h7 ♖h1+ 11 ♔g6 ♖g1+ 12 ♔h7 ♔f7) 9...♖g1+ 10 ♔f7 and White saves the game. (2 points)

7) Passed pawns are often decisive in queen endings. White should not delay the c5 breakthrough since otherwise Black will play ...♕d6, when c5 can be met by ...♕xc5. **1 c5! bxc5 2 b6 ♕b8 3 b7 c4** (Black tries to get some counterplay with his c-pawn) **4 ♕b6** (the manoeuvre ♕b6-c6-c8 is typical for queen endings) **4...c3 5 ♕c6 ♔h7 6 ♕c8 ♕a7 7 ♔g2** (7 b8♕? is too hasty and allows a perpetual check by 7...♕xf2+ 8 ♔h3 ♕f1+) **7...c2** (or else b8♕ wins at once) **8 ♕xc2+ ♔h8 9 ♕c8+** and b8♕, with an extra queen. (2 points for finding **1 c5!**)

8) After 1 ♖b7? ♖c8+ 2 ♔d4 ♖c1 Black activates his rook and draws, while 1 ♔c5? ♔e7! 2 ♖b7+ ♔d7 3 ♖b8 ♖c7+ is also a draw as the black king can move in front of the d-pawn. **1 ♖e1!** is the key move, cutting off the black king along the e-file. After **1...♖c8+ 2 ♔b5 ♖d8 3 ♔c6 ♖c8+ 4 ♔d7 ♖a8** (4...♖c2 5 d6 will lead to the Lucena position even more quickly) **5**

d6 罝a7+ 6 畳c8 罝a8+ 7 畳b7 罝a2 8 d7 罝b2+ 9 畳c7 罝c2+ 10 畳d8 White reaches the Lucena position – see Exercise 25 on page 58. (3 points for finding **1 罝e1!**)

9) 1...畳e4? loses to 2 g6 followed by g7, while 1...畳f8? stops the pawns but allows White to win by 2 畳d7 畳e4 3 畳e8 畳a3 4 g6. **1...畳e3!** is the only move to draw. It might seem odd to force White to push his pawn to h7, but this allows Black to blockade the pawns. After **2 h7 畳d4 3 畳d7 畳e4 4 畳e6 畳f4 5 g6 畳g5 6 畳f7 畳h6** Black's king makes it back just in time to cover g7, with a safe draw. (3 points for finding **1...畳e3!**)

10) After **1...a3**, the only way to win is **2 b3!** (2 bxa3? 畳e7 is drawn because a rook's pawn is always a draw if the defending king can get in front of the pawn, while 2 b4? 畳e7 3 畳a2 畳d6 4 畳xa3 畳c6 5 畳a4 畳b6 is a draw as in Exercise 8 on page 17) **2...畳e7 3 畳a2 畳d6 4 畳xa3 畳c5 5 畳a4! 畳b6** (5...畳c6 6 畳a5 畳b7 7 畳b5 畳a7 8 畳c6 is also winning) **6 畳b4** and White has the opposition, as in Exercise 7 on page 17. (3 points for finding **2 b3!**, and 1 more for seeing the rest of the main line)

Test Paper 3

11) By using his king to lift the stalemate, White can move his king down the board with gain of time: **1 畳g6! 畳g2 2 畳f5+ 畳f1** (now the king is close enough for White to win using the mating attack method of Exercise 7 on page 85) **3 營a1+ 畳g2 4 營b2+ 畳g1** (the queen is ideally placed on the second rank, and the white king moves in for the kill) **5 畳g4 h1營 6 畳g3** and Black can only delay mate for a few moves by giving up his queen. (2 points for finding **1 畳g6!**)

12) 1 畳d5? 畳d7 2 畳c5 畳c7 is only a draw because Black can always oppose the white king and prevent it from advancing to the sixth rank. **1 畳c5!** wins because it gains the opposition and ensures that White will win the black pawn; for example, **1...畳d7 2 畳d5 畳e7 3 畳c6 畳e8** (however Black plays, he is gradually pushed back) **4 畳d6 畳f7 5 畳d7 畳f8 6 畳e6 畳g7 7 畳e7 畳g8 8 畳xf6 畳f8** with the standard win of Exercise 6 on page 16. (2 points for finding **1 畳c5!**)

13) Recall that it's better for the defender to have the bishop that does not control the corner square (here a1), so it's the bishop on f1 that Black needs to keep. 1...畳a2? is wrong because after 2 罝xf1 Black has the 'wrong' bishop and White wins as in the right-hand diagram on page 72: 2...畳h2 3 罝h1 畳g3 4 罝h6 畳a3 5 罝h3. **1...畳c4!** is the only move by the f1-bishop that prevents 罝a3# and after 2 罝xf4 畳e6 we have the draw of Exercise 4 on page 74. (2 points)

14) 1 畳f8? loses to 1...畳f6!, which allows Black to edge closer to a2 without releasing the white king from the back rank. Then 2 畳g8 畳e5 3 畳f7 畳d4 4 畳e6 畳c3 5 畳d5 畳b2 6 畳c4 畳xa2 7 畳c3 畳b1 is one move too slow and Black wins. **1 畳h8!** is the drawing move, so that if Black makes a run for the a-pawn, White can meet ...畳xa2 with 畳c2; for example, **1...畳f5 2 畳g7 畳e4 3 畳f6 畳d3 4 畳e5 畳c2 5 畳d4 畳b2 6 畳d3 畳xa2 7 畳c2** and the king arrives just in time. (3 points)

15) White will win if he can reach b7 with his king, as then he will be sheltered from black rook checks. With the pawn defended by the king, White's rook will be free to become active. 1 畳e3? loses a move and allows Black to draw by 1...畳f7 2 畳d4 畳e7 3 畳c5 畳d7, when the white king cannot reach b7. 1 b7? removes the possible shelter for the white king and the position is then a clear draw (see Exercise 21 on page 57). The winning move is **1 ♔e4!**. After **1...♖b5** (Black tries to prevent the king from reaching b7; 1...♔f7 2 ♔d5 ♔e7 3 ♔c6 is also losing for Black) **2 ♔d4 ♔f7 3 ♔c4 ♖b1 4 ♔c5 ♔e7 5 ♔c6** White is just in time to reach b7. (3 points for **1 ♔e4!**)

16) If the black king moves to the d-file then White promotes with check after 2 d7 ♘e5 3 d8♕+, while 1...♔e2? 2 d7 ♘e5 3 ♘d4+ followed by d8♕ prevents the knight fork on c6 and wins. 1...♔f1? 2 ♘e3+! ♔xe3 3 d7 drags the black knight away and promotes the pawn without allowing a fork. **1...♔f2!** is the only move to draw. After **2 d7 ♘e5** (2...♘a5? 3 ♘d4 ♘b7 4 ♘b3 ♔e3 5 ♘c5 ♘a5 6 ♔d6 ♘c4+ 7 ♔e6 ensures promotion of the pawn) **3 d8♕ ♘c6+** Black eliminates the queen. (3 points for **1...♔f2!** and 2 points for the rest of the main line)

Test Paper 4

17) After 1 h4? ♔d6 2 h5 ♔e6 3 h6 ♔f6 4 h7 ♔g7 Black is in time to catch the pawn. Rather than just pushing the pawn, White must use his king to block the black king's route to h8: **1 ♔e5! ♔d7 2 ♔f6 ♔e8 3 ♔g7** and now the pawn can advance in safety; for example, **3...♔e7 4 h4 ♔e6 5 h5**. (1 point for **1 ♔e5!**)

18) 1...♔h5? 2 ♔d4 ♔g4 3 ♔e3 ♔g3 4 ♔e2 wins for White; for example, 4...♔h3 5 ♔f3 ♔h2 6 ♔f2 ♔h3 7 ♖xd2 ♔h2 8 ♖d1 ♔h3 9 ♖g1 and White takes both pawns. **1...♔g5!** leads to a draw after **2 ♔d4 ♔f4!** (it's the shouldering-away idea again: Black uses his own king to keep the white king out) **3 ♔d3 ♔f3 4 ♔xd2 ♔f2** and Black will win the rook. (2 points for **1...♔g5! 2 ♔d4 ♔f4!**)

19) If White can stop Black's checks then he will win with his far-advanced f-pawn. 1 ♔a4? ♕e4+ 2 ♔b5 ♕f5+ gives Black too many checks, while 1 ♔b2? ♕f2+ 2 ♔b3 ♔h5! followed by ...♔g6 attacks the pawn and draws (note that the queen on f2 stops 3 ♕c5+). **1 ♔b4!** is the only way to win. After 1...♕e4+ or 1...♕g4+ White plays 2 ♕c4, pinning the black queen. If Black does not check but plays 1...♕f6, to prevent ♕e7+ followed by f8♕, then 2 ♕c4+ followed by ♕c5+ (promoting the pawn) or ♕c3+ (exchanging queens) wins quickly. (2 points)

20) 1 ♔b5? ♔b7 2 ♖h1 is only a draw after 2...♖g8 (2...♖h8, playing for stalemate, is also good) 3 ♖h7+ ♔b8 (see Exercise 32 on page 59), and 1 ♖h1? ♖a8+ 2 ♔b5 ♖a2 activates the black rook and draws after 3 ♖h8+ ♔b7 4 ♖h7+ ♔b8 5 ♔c6 ♖c2+, checking the white king away. **1 ♖c1+!** is the only move to win, based on the tactical point **1...♔b7 2 ♖c7+ ♔a8 3 ♖a7#**. If instead 1...♔d7, then Black's king is cut off from the b-pawn and 2 ♔a6 ♖a8+ 3 ♔b7 ♖a2 4 ♔b8 followed by b7 leads to the Lucena position – see Exercise 25 on page 58. (3 points)

21) The obvious 1 h6? is surprisingly met by 1...♔d5! 2 h7 ♘e5+ 3 ♔e7 ♘g6+ 4 ♔f6 ♘h8 5 ♔g7 ♔e6 6 ♔xh8 ♔f7 and Black is just in time to box the white king in. **1 ♔e6!** is the way to keep the black knight out, and after **1...♘d6 2 h6 ♘e4 3 ♔f5!** (the same idea again: keeping the knight out is more important than pushing the pawn; 3 h7? loses the pawn after 3...♘g5+) **3...♘d6+ 4 ♔g6** the pawn will promote. (2 points for **1 ♔e6!** and 2 more for finding the main line up to **3 ♔f5!**)

22) Black just needs to cover g8 with his bishop, but that is easier said than done. 1...♗c7+? 2 ♔e5! (2 ♔d4? ♔d6 3 g7 ♗d5 draws) and 1...♔b6+? 2 ♔d4! (2 ♔e5? ♔c5 3 g7 ♗d5 draws) win for White as in both cases the black bishop cannot stop the pawn. **1...♗c6!** is better as the king retains the option of moving to d6 or c5. Then **2 ♗a3** (White plays to prevent both ...♔d6 and ...♔c5; 2 ♔e5 ♔c5 and 2 ♔d4 ♔d6 are clearly drawn) **2...♔d7+!** (Black can no longer control g8 with his bishop, but now his king is near enough to head for g8 instead) **3 ♔e5 ♔e8! 4 ♔e6** (to prevent Black from meeting g7 with ...♗f7) **4...♗e4!** (the roles switch again and it's the bishop that finally stops the pawn) **5 g7 ♗h7** draws. (2 points for **1...♗c6!**, 2 more for finding **2 ♗a3 ♔d7+!** and a bonus 1 point for the rest of the main line)

Test Paper 5

23) Despite being a pawn down, White can win with the neat tactic **1 ♕h4+! ♔xh4** (otherwise Black loses his queen) **2 ♘f3#.** (2 points)

24) It looks as if both moves win, but one of them falls into a subtle trap. 1 ♔g3? is met by 1...h4+ and it's stalemate after 2 ♔h3 ♔h1! 3 ♖xg2 or 2 ♔f3 h3 3 ♖a1+ ♔h2 4 ♔f2 g1♕+ 5 ♖xg1. **1 ♔f3!** is the winning move, picking up the g-pawn without allowing stalemate. Then it's an easy win; for example, 1...h4 2 ♖xg2+ ♔h1 3 ♔f2 h3 4 ♖g1+ ♔h2 5 ♖g3 ♔h1 6 ♖xh3#. (2 points)

25) White needs something special since once Black retrieves his wayward knight the position is drawn: **1 ♗d6+!** (the bishop is heading for b4, where it imprisons the knight) **1...♔f7 2 ♗b4! ♔e6 3 ♔d4** (Black is in zugzwang and must give way with his king) **3...♔d7 4 ♔d5 ♔d8 5 e6 ♔e8** (this would be a draw without the bishop and knight, but White can use his bishop's control of e7 to win the game) **6 ♔e5! ♔d8** (in a pure pawn ending Black would play ...♔e7 to draw, but here the bishop controls e7) **7 ♔f6 ♔e8 8 e7 ♔d7 9 ♔f7** and White wins. (2 points for finding **1 ♗d6+!** and **2 ♗b4!**)

26) It's not enough just to win Black's rook for the c-pawn; for example, after 1 ♔d7? g5 2 c8♕? (2 ♖e8 still draws) 2...♖xc8 3 ♔xc8 g4 Black even wins with his connected passed pawns. The correct line is **1 ♖e5+!** (playing the rook to c5 means that White gets a whole queen for the c-pawn and not just a rook) **1...g5** (Black doesn't have a good square for his king, since 1...♔g4 2 ♖c5 ♖xc5 3 ♔xc5 h2 4 c8♕+ promotes with check, while after 1...♔h4 2 ♖c5 or 1...♔h6 2 ♖c5 White wins as in the main line) **2 ♖c5 ♖xc5** (2...h2 3 c8♕ ♖xc5 4 ♕h3+ ♔g6 5 ♔xc5 is an easy win) **3 ♔xc5 h2 4 c8♕ h1♕ 5 ♕h8+** and the skewer wins the black queen. (2 points for **1 ♖e5+!** and 1 extra for the rest of the main line)

27) Black's threat is ...d4 followed by ...d3+ and to prevent this White must cover d3 with his bishop. There are apparently two ways to do this: one is to put the bishop on b5 or a6, and the other is to put it on c2. However, 1 ♗b5? d4 2 ♗a6 loses because Black can play his king to c3; for example, 2...♔d6 3 ♗b5 (White's bishop cannot move away from b5 or a6 or else Black plays ...d3+ at once) 3...♔c5 4 ♗a6 ♔b4 followed by ...♔c3 and ...d3+. **1 ♗a4! d4 2 ♗c2!** is the way to do it. White again prevents ...d3+, but also attacks the pawn on e4 so that Black cannot play his king round to c3. Now it's a clear draw. (3 points)

28) **1 ♔d4!** (the 'shouldering away' idea is combined with an eventual skewer; 1 ♔d5? a5 2 c4 a4 3 ♔d4 a3 4 ♔c3 ♔e4 and 1 ♔b5? ♔e4 2 c4 ♔e5 3 c5 ♔d5! 4 c6 ♔d6 only draw) **1...♔f4**

123

(1...a5 2 c4 a4 3 c5 a3 4 ♔c3 is also winning) **2 c4 ♔f5 3 ♔d5 ♔f6** (White wins after 3...a5 4 c5 a4 5 c6 since he promotes with check) **4 ♔d6 a5** (after 4...♔f7 5 c5 ♔e8 6 ♔c7 a5 7 c6 a4 8 ♔b7 White also promotes with check) **5 c5 a4 6 c6 a3 7 c7 a2 8 c8♕ a1♕ 9 ♕h8+** and White wins the queen. (2 points for **1 ♔d4!** and 3 more for finding the rest of the main line)

Test Paper 6

29) **1...♔f7?** loses to **2 ♖h8!** (threatening 3 a8♕) **2...♖xa7 3 ♖h7+**, and **1...♖b6+?** to **2 ♔c4 ♖a6 3 ♖f8+**. **1...♔g7!** is the only move to draw. One line runs **2 ♔b4** (with the king on g7 there is no skewer, so White tries to advance his king) **2...♖a1 3 ♔b5 ♖h7 4 ♔b6** (now White threatens to move his rook, so Black starts checking) **4...♖b1+ 5 ♔c7 ♖c1+** and so on. (1 point for **1...♔g7!**)

30) Queen against bishop's pawn on the seventh is normally a draw, so if Black can play ...♔d2 he will be safe. White must prevent this, while at the same time stopping Black from promoting. There's only one move that achieves both aims: **1 ♕g2!**. Then 1...c1♕ 2 ♕g5+ wins the new queen with a skewer, while after 1...♔d3 2 ♕g5 followed by ♕c1 White permanently blockades the pawn and can bring his king up for a win. (2 points)

31) Checking in the distant corner is the only winning move: **1 ♕a8+!** (1 ♕xf2? is stalemate, 1 ♕b1+? ♕g1+! forces a queen swap and 1 ♕d5+? ♔h2 is a draw because White has no check on the h-file) **1...♔h2** (1...♔g1 2 ♘h3+ wins the queen) **2 ♕h8+!** (White makes good use of the corners of the board) **2...♔g1** (or 2...♔g3 3 ♕h3#) **3 ♘h3+** and the queen falls to a knight fork. (2 points)

32) Cutting the black king off along a rank is even more effective than cutting it off along a file. The only winning move is **1 ♖h6!** (other moves allow the black king to move closer to the white pawn; for example, 1 c5? ♔d5 or 1 ♔b5? ♔d6) **1...♖b8+ 2 ♔c5 ♖c8+ 3 ♔b5 ♖b8+ 4 ♖b6** (the rook can shield the white king from checks while maintaining control of the sixth rank to prevent Black's king from approaching) **4...♖h8 5 c5** and there's nothing Black can do to prevent the pawn from edging forwards. The continuation might be **5...♖h1 6 ♖g6 ♔f5 7 ♖d6 ♔e5 8 ♔b6 ♖b1+ 9 ♔c7 ♖h1 10 c6 ♖h7+ 11 ♖d7 ♖h1 12 ♖d2** (there are many ways to win, but switching to a cut-off along a file is perhaps the simplest) **12...♔e6 13 ♔b7 ♖b1+ 14 ♔c8** and White will soon arrive at the Lucena position. (3 points for **1 ♖h6!**)

33) White must drive the enemy bishop off the a4-e8 diagonal so that he can advance the pawn, but he should not block his own pawn in the process. 1 ♗c4? is bad because after 1...♗d2 2 ♗b5 ♗h5 White must move his bishop before he can push the pawn, which gives Black time to defend. After 3 ♗c6 ♗e2 4 ♗d5 ♔c3, Black prevents ♗c4 and so White will never be able to advance the pawn. The winning line is **1 ♗d5! ♔d2 2 ♗c6** (driving away the bishop without blocking the pawn) **2...♗h5 3 b5 ♗g4 4 b6 ♗c8** (this last-ditch defence only delays the end) **5 ♔d6 ♔c3 6 ♔c7 ♗a6 7 ♗b5** (7 ♗d7 followed by ♗c8 also wins) **7...♗xb5 8 b7** and White promotes the pawn. (3 points for **1 ♗d5!**)

34) This exercise shows that the opposition is important not only in pawn endings. 1 ♔f7? ♔f5! is a draw, as Black keeps opposing the white king: 2 ♔g7 ♔g5! 3 ♔f7 ♔f5 and so on. If White ever plays ♖f2, for example 4 ♖f2 here, then Black gains time by attacking the rook with a later ...♔e3. This allows him to draw by 4...♔e4 5 ♔f6 ♔e3 6 ♖a2 f3 7 ♔e5 f2 8

♖a1 ♔e2. 1 ♔d7? is also wrong and leads to a draw after 1...♔e4 2 ♔e6 f3 3 ♔f6 ♔e3 4 ♔g5 ♔e2. **1 ♔e7!** is the only move to win, gaining the opposition. Then **1...♔f5** (after 1...♔e4 2 ♔f6 f3 3 ♔g5 ♔e3 4 ♔g4 f2 5 ♔g3 White wins the pawn) **2 ♔f7!** ♔e4 (2...♔g4 3 ♔e6 is a mirror image) **3 ♔g6 f3 4 ♔g5 ♔e3 5 ♔g4 f2 6 ♔g3** leads to the capture of the pawn. In order to win, White's king must run up the board on the opposite side of the pawn to Black's king. White can only achieve this if he gains the opposition. (3 points for **1 ♔e7!** and 2 more for finding **1...♔f5 2 ♔f7!**)

Test Paper 7

35) If Black can get his pawn to f2 he will draw, but only one king move achieves this. After 1...♔g2? 2 ♕a8 ♔g3 3 ♔f6 White wins easily because 3...f2 4 ♕h1 permanently blocks the pawn. Also, not 1...♔e2? 2 ♕e8+! (White must avoid 2 ♕e7+? ♔f1, when there are no more checks) 2...♔f1 3 ♕b5+ ♔g1 4 ♕b1+ ♔g2 5 ♕e4 and again the diagonal pin is decisive. **1...♔f1!** is correct. White has no checks and so cannot prevent ...f2, with the draw of Exercise 2 on page 84. (2 points)

36) In view of Black's far-advanced pawn, the only way to win is by the tactical trick **1 ♖f8!**, so that 1...♖xh7 loses to 2 ♔g6+ ♔e2 3 ♔xh7 followed by ♖a8. The best defence is **1...a2 2 h8♕ a1♕** and, as usual when both kings are totally exposed, whoever has the first check wins. Almost any check wins for White, but the simplest method is **3 ♔e4+ ♔e1** (or 3...♔e2 4 ♕h2+ ♔e1 5 ♕g3+ ♔d2 6 ♖f2+) **4 ♕h1+ ♔d2 5 ♕h2+ ♔c3 6 ♖c8+ ♔b4 7 ♕b8+** followed by **♕xa7+**. (2 points for **1 ♖f8!**)

37) White has the rook's pawn plus wrong bishop combination, so Black might be able to draw if can give up his bishop for the g-pawn. The problem is that the immediate 1...♗c8+? 2 ♔g5 ♗xg4 doesn't work because White plays 3 hxg4 and no longer has a rook's pawn. Similarly, 1...♗e2? 2 g5 followed by h4 keeps the g-pawn and wins. The drawing line is **1...♗f1! 2 h4** (forced, as otherwise Black just takes the h-pawn) **2...♗h3!**, pinning the g-pawn so that it cannot advance to g5. Next move Black plays ...♗xg4+, eliminating the g-pawn, leaving a clear draw. (2 points)

38) There are no winning chances once Black plays ...c5 and controls the pawn's queening square, so White must prevent the c-pawn from advancing: **1 ♘e6+! ♔e5 2 ♘c5 ♔d6** (there's no way for the bishop to stop the pawn) **3 a6 ♗c7** (3...♗xc5 4 a7 is also hopeless for Black) **4 a7** followed by **a8♕**, winning. (2 points for finding **1 ♘e6+!** followed by **2 ♘c5**)

39) White needs to have his rook behind the passed g-pawn, which will force Black to blockade it with his rook. However, Black is threatening 1...♖d2+ followed by ...♖g2, putting his own rook behind the pawn, and to prevent this White needs to play **1 ♖e2!**, heading for g2. One line runs **1...♖g7 2 ♖g2 ♖g6 3 ♔b2 ♔c6 4 ♔c3 ♔d5 5 ♔b4 ♔c6 6 ♔c4 ♔d6 7 b4 ♔c6 8 ♖g1** (Black is now in zugzwang: a rook move allows the g-pawn to advance, and otherwise he must either play ...b5+ or allow the white king to reach b5) **8...♔d6** (8...b5+ 9 ♔d4 ♔d6 10 ♖g2 is another zugzwang, when Black must allow either ♔c5 or ♔e5) **9 ♔b5 ♔c7 10 ♔a6 ♔b8 11 b5 ♔a8 12 ♖f1** (now that White's king and b-pawn are so far advanced, he can switch his rook around) **12...♔b8 13 ♖f5 ♔c7 14 ♔a7 ♖g7 15 ♖f6 ♖xg5 16 ♖c6+ ♔d7 17 ♔xb6** and White will soon reach the Lucena position. (3 points for **1 ♖e2!**)

40) White wins by **1 f5!** ♔**g5** (after 1...♔g3 2 f6 h4 3 f7 h3 4 f8♕ h2 5 ♕f1 White can simply approach with his king) **2 ♔e5!** (2 ♔e6? allows Black to escape after 2...h4 3 f6 h3 4 f7 h2 5 f8♕ h1♕ 6 ♕g7+ ♔f4) **2...h4 3 f6 ♔g6** (3...h3 4 f7 h2 5 f8♕ h1♕ 6 ♕g7+ and ♕h7+ wins the black queen) **4 ♔e6 h3 5 f7 h2 6 f8♕ h1♕ 7 ♕g8+** followed by ♕**h8+**, winning the queen with a skewer. (1 point for **1 f5!**, 2 more for **2 ♔e5!** and a bonus point for seeing the rest of the main line)

Test Paper 8

41) 1 ♔c5+? ♔f3 2 ♔d4 g3 3 ♖a3+ ♔f2 4 ♔e4 g2 5 ♖a2+ ♔g3 6 ♖a1 ♔h2 draws, as does 1 ♖a8? g3 2 ♔c3 g2 3 ♖g8 ♔f3 4 ♔d2 ♔f2. **1 ♔c3+!** is the way to stop Black's pawn; for example, **1...♔f3 2 ♔d2! g3 3 ♔e1! g2** (3...♔g2 4 ♔e2 ♔h2 5 ♖g4 g2 6 ♔f2 is also winning for White) **4 ♖a3+!** followed by ♔f2 and the pawn falls. (2 points for **1 ♔c3+!**)

42) Black is threatening to play ...♔d4 and ...♘d3, when he would be safe, so White must act at once: **1 ♖c3!** (1 ♔c5? ♔e4 draws) **1...♘a2** (after 1...♘e2 2 ♖e3+ White wins the knight) **2 ♖c4!** (immobilizing the knight and cutting off the black king, which can no longer come to the knight's aid) **2...♔e6** (it doesn't matter where Black moves his king) **3 ♔c5 ♔e5 4 ♖c2** and the knight is lost. (1 point for **1 ♖c3!** and another point for **1...♘a2 2 ♖c4!**)

43) Black can only draw by **1...♘f4! 2 b6 ♘e6!** (not 2...♘d5? 3 b7 ♘b4 4 ♔b6! ♘d5+ 5 ♔c6 ♘b4+ 6 ♔b5 and the pawn promotes) **3 b7 ♘d8!** (3...♘d4? loses to 4 ♔b6) **4 b8♕ ♘c6+**, picking up the queen. (2 points)

44) White needs the help of his king to win, and it turns out that the king needs to be on d6. There's only one way to reach d6 in two moves, and anything slower doesn't win. **1 ♔e7! ♖c5** (Black executes his threat; after other moves White plays ♔d6 and wins easily once his king is supporting the pawns) **2 ♔d6! ♖xb5 3 c7** (the rook cannot return to c5 when the king is on d6, so to prevent immediate promotion Black must check) **3...♖b6+ 4 ♔d5** (now White wins as in Exercise 13 on page 56) **4...♖b5+ 5 ♔d4** (5 ♔c4? ♖b1! allows Black to escape) **5...♖b4+ 6 ♔d3** (6 ♔c3 ♖b1 7 ♔c2 is just as good) **6...♖b3+ 7 ♔c2** and White wins as promotion cannot be delayed any further. (2 points for finding the main line up to **3 c7** and 1 bonus point for working out how to avoid the checks)

45) 1 ♔xb3+? is bad as 1...♔d5 brings Black's king too close to the white pawn for a win. 1 ♕e7+? ♔f3! 2 ♕f6+ ♔e2! is also only a draw. The check on b7 is better because it prevents Black's king from running away via f3 and e2: **1 ♕b7+! ♔f4** (best, since 1...♔e3 2 ♕b6+ costs Black his queen, while 1...♔e5 2 ♕d5+ followed by ♕d4+ and 1...♔f2 2 ♕d5+ followed by ♕d4+ or ♕g8+ lead to a queen swap or a skewer) **2 ♕f7+! ♔e5** (2...♔e4 3 ♕d5+ is the same) **3 ♕d5+**, followed by ♕d4+, exchanging queens into a winning pawn ending. (3 points)

46) After 1 ♔e6? both sides promote and it is a draw; for example, 1...b4 2 f6 b3 3 f7 b2 4 f8♕ b1♕ 5 ♕a8+ ♔b3 6 ♕b7+ ♔c2. White must play **1 ♔e5!** to draw Black's king into a position which allows White to promote with check. After **1...b4 2 ♔d4 b3 3 ♔c3 ♔a3 4 f6 b2 5 f7 b1♕** (even though Black promotes first, White promotes with check and wins thanks to the poor position of Black's king) **6 f8♕+ ♔a4** (6...♔a2 7 ♕a8#) **7 ♕a8+ ♔b5 8 ♕b7+** (or 8 ♕b8+) White wins the black queen with a skewer. (2 points for **1 ♔e5!** and 2 more for finding the rest of the main line)

Score-Chart

Test number	Maximum score	Your score
1	7	
2	15	
3	17	
4	17	
5	17	
6	16	
7	15	
8	16	
Total	120	

Rate your score:

0-20   Revision necessary!

21-45   Focus on your weaker areas

46-70   Shows potential

71-90   Promising talent

91-100   Potential international player

101-110 Potential Master strength

111-120 Potential Grandmaster

FORTRESS

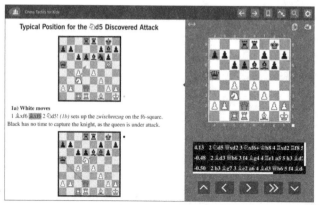